Collins

need to know?

How to read a building

Timothy Brittain-Catlin

Collins

First published in 2007 by Collins
an imprint of
HarperCollins Publishers
77-85 Fulham Palace Road
London W6 8JB

www.collins.co.uk

Til Jonathan Rauhe Pedersen

A catalogue record for this book is available from the
British Library

Managing editor: Louise Stanley
Designer: Pascal Thivillon, Basement Press
Proofreading: Nicola Chalton, Basement Press
Series design: Mark Thomson
Front cover photograph: © Andy Marshall/Alamy
Back cover photographs: © (from left to right)
Dave Lidwell/Alamy, Versha Jones and WidStock/Alamy

ISBN-10: 0-00-724746-X
ISBN-13: 978-0-00-724746-2

Printed and bound by Printing Express Ltd, Hong Kong

Contents

Architecture is for everyone

Architecture is everywhere: it is part of our lives, and its continuing development is a central theme in the history of mankind. Learning to read a building is the route to understanding a major part of our cultural inheritance.

must know
Great architects
The greatest architects of the western world created buildings that are not only international icons but have also come to symbolize the culture of a city and its people. London would be unthinkable without Sir Christopher Wren's St Paul's Cathedral, Sydney without Jørn Utzon's opera house, or Paris without Charles Garnier's opera house and Hector Guimard's art nouveau Metro stations.

Whether you live in a small flat or a detached house, you can find traces of architectural history all around you. Architecture is not just about style, although historical styles have made buildings memorable and beautiful for hundreds of years. Architecture is the sum of many small parts, some as small as a door or a window, as well as being the general term for the study of why people choose to build the way they do. Learning to read buildings starts with enjoying architectural details and discovering how much pleasure can be derived from looking around you and understanding your own environment.

The first thing we can all do when embarking on a discovery of architecture is to try to analyse what we see in a room we know well. Are the doors flush or panelled? How do the windows open? Is there a plaster cornice, or a decorative skirting board? Is there a consistent pattern to the features inside the house? How does the layout of the rooms work? Even if these are the same as they are in the flat or house next door, they will very probably make a statement about what sort of home we live in, and how that home relates to the story of architecture as a whole. After all, an outline of architectural history will only make sense if it is broad enough to include the majority of buildings we all live and work in.

With experience and enthusiasm it becomes possible to classify visual ideas into clear stylistic traditions which govern the form of every part of a building from its general outline to its detail. These common patterns are the major historical traditions, in particular the 'classical' and the 'gothic'; both styles have roots in a series of important historical buildings which have long influenced architects and artists, and anyone interested in the subject must know what they are.

Buildings are not only about style, however: they are also a record of the way in which people have lived and worked in the past. The choice of a building material, or a type of chimney or roof tile, may be related to local resources. The way in which craftsmen have worked and finished those materials is often a sign of the natural characteristics of the materials themselves. To some extent therefore one can say that when a region of a country has developed a very distinct way of building because of the types of materials and skills prevalent there, we have an example of a further and unique type of style. Indeed, some of our most memorable buildings have resulted from the combination of a local style with one of the great international traditions of formal architecture. Your own home is unlikely, of course, to satisfy your own curiosity. The centre of your nearest town, however, will almost certainly bear witness to the major traditions of architecture. It is quite possible that there may be a church or a public building there that testifies to an important phase of national architecture. At all events, you will soon start to uncover fascinating aspects of architectural style and history from the buildings that you pass every day.

1 The elements of architecture

Evidence of the great historical styles of the past is all around us. Whoever built your home was working within a tradition – even if at first sight it might seem as though there is nothing special about it. For every house, in every style, belongs to the developing history of architecture. With careful analysis of what you see every day, you can step into the world of architectural history, and begin to appreciate the many beauties of the buildings of our towns and cities.

Analysing your home

The first step towards understanding architectural history is to analyse exactly what you see around you. What are the major component parts that your house is made of? What do they look like, and how were they put together?

Walls and roofs

If your house is built with plain brick or plastered walls, the chances are that you have never given them much thought. And yet these are the most important parts of any home. The purpose of a house from the beginning of time has been to build somewhere that is protected from the elements. The very first houses were shelters created out of whatever material was available. In England, with its dense woodlands, sections of tree trunks were tied together to form a rigid tent, and its surface was covered with woven twigs and leaves. Sometimes walls were built up using mud and clay. Once sturdier materials could be moved from place to place, the first upright masonry walls began to appear.

The wall and the roof are still the most important elements in architecture, and very probably their appearance was the first thing that the builder of your house decided on.

The walls

Step outside your home and look carefully at the surface of the outer walls:
- is it made of timber?
- is it made of brick?

must know
Wattle and daub
The walls of old timber-framed buildings were often filled in with wattle and daub. Wattle refers to a wickerwork infill built of rods and twigs, and daub was a coating made of clay, dung, horsehair and other materials. Wattle and daub panels were then usually plastered.

- is it made of stone?
- is it covered in plaster, or render?
- is it made from a concrete frame?

The location of your house may well account for the material of the outer face of the walls. It is only comparatively recently in the history of architecture – for most people, less than two hundred years – that it has been economically viable to move heavy building materials around the country. Well into the twentieth century such expensive transportation was still avoided if possible. That means that in most cases the surface of the walls will be made from a material that can be found locally. If you live in a more recent home, you need only look at the fronts of older buildings to get a clear idea of what the local building material is.

Timber walls

Walls built with timber frames are comparatively rare in Britain, although many have survived from hundreds of years ago. Originally, numerous houses were built with timber frames and covered with timber clapboarding, but as brick and stone became increasingly available, and because the priority in a wet country was to keep warm and dry, the timber cladding was often later replaced with brick. On the other hand, when English settlers arrived in the Americas in the sixteenth and seventeenth centuries, they found plentiful supplies of timber which could be easily felled and worked. The result was a style of architecture which has remained popular ever since, especially on the east coast of the United States.

Builders traditionally used local building materials, which accounts for the wonderful variety of brick and stone in our houses. This modern house echoes that tradition.

English settlers in the New World used plentiful local timber to build in a way that was familiar from home.

A timber frame with timber cladding is not necessarily inferior to masonry construction. Units can be prefabricated and transferred quickly and cheaply to site, and because of their natural appearance can easily blend in with any other local material. Nowadays, thermal insulation standards can be met with thick layers of mineral wool or other modern materials, and so the protective properties of the external layer are less important than they were traditionally. In fact, the Nordic countries with their plentiful forests make great use of timber-framed, timber-clad structures for modern high-quality housing, and it is likely that their use will spread.

Brick and stone

The most solid building materials are found under
the earth. In Britain, there is a large selection of
stones and clays which have provided a
tremendous variety of building materials. In the
south-east of the country, around London, the clay
is just right for making bricks, and so for many
people who have seen the characteristic rows of
houses in the capital, England is a country of brick.
But there is also a long belt of limestone that
stretches across the land from Dorset in the south-
west up to Yorkshire in the north-east. This
provides the varied and attractive stones that
characterize the architecture of much of the centre
of the country. There are also coloured sandstones
in the west and north-west.

Because the wall is the most important part of
any house, builders will have to adapt their work to
the natural properties of the material. Brick can be
cast into small units. Most limestones can be
easily cut and carved into blocks, sometimes into
the largest units that can be comfortably
manoeuvred into place by a mason working alone.
And because the dense granites of the far north

and west of the country are so difficult to cut and so inconvenient to move around on a building site, the architecture of those regions is correspondingly plain and massive.

must know

Limestone

Many stone buildings in England are built of limestone, which basically consists of calcium carbonate. It was formed between 70 and 345 million years ago, and comes in several forms, from soft chalk to a kind of marble. All limestone is sedimentary and formed into layers or strata; and it contains much fossilized matter.

must know

Sandstone

Sandstone is also a sedimentary rock. It is composed of hardwearing quartz or other minerals held together by a cementing material such as silica or calcite. The magnificent Anglican cathedral in Liverpool is built of vibrant local red sandstone.

Most kinds of limestone used in building are well suited for decorative carving.

Rendered walls

Quarrying and working with stone is always going to be a relatively expensive part of the building process, and yet in many countries the local clay is not suitable for making good quality wind- and rainproof bricks. The solution is to cover a wall with a thick mix of plaster, properly known as render, usually based on gypsum or more commonly lime mixed with other materials including sand or gravel. In some areas, including for example those parts of Scotland where an expensive granite is the local natural building material, one can see a great deal of housing built of cheap bricks or blocks which are protected against the rain by a thick layer of render.

Although a rendered wall is therefore a comparatively cheaper solution, it does have many advantages. It can be painted in cheerful colours, and in some parts of England, especially East Anglia, the surface was often decorated by pressing it when wet with patterned wooden moulds. This is known as pargetting.

Concrete walls

Concrete walls – usually, in fact, concrete frames with panels made from other materials – are the result of

must know

Ashlar and rubble _stonework_

Ashlar is the name used for masonry built up from stone cut into neat, rectangular blocks. Rubble refers to rough, unfinished stone construction. Rubble walls can consist of stone randomly placed, or of irregular stones placed roughly in courses.

must know

Concrete

The Romans used concrete, but its popularity today is due to the fact that it can be moulded into any shape and is relatively tough. It is made by mixing sand, cement, and an aggregate (crushed stone or gravel). Reinforced concrete is made by pouring the concrete mix over a network of iron bars. The high thermal mass of concrete – which can store heat – and the fact that existing concrete structures can often be comparatively easily refurbished to some extent balance the ecological problems generated by its manufacture.

architectural fashion rather than of natural circumstances. If you live in a building such as a block of flats from the 1950s or 1960s where you can clearly see large amounts of concrete, the chances are that you are daily experiencing the conscious attempt of an architect to get involved with the design experimentation that was going on at the time. In order to understand your building best, you need to stand back and look at the block as a whole, and to try to understand its logic. Chapter 5 of this book will give you an insight into what effects architects at the time were trying to achieve with work of this type.

Roofs

A building will not keep the rain out without a roof. In a warm climate with little rain a flat roof may well be completely adequate, for water will dry out before it becomes a problem. In northern countries, however, builders and architects have right from the start tried to design roofs that will direct rainwater away from the building as soon as possible. The heavier the rainfall, the steeper the roof, and the deeper the overhang of the roof over the top of the wall.

must know
Roofs
Many materials can be used for cladding roofs. In clay areas they are traditionally covered with tiles, but they have also been made of stone, of lead, or of thatch.
'Green' roofs made of turf are increasingly popular because they reduce the environmental impact of a new building while providing excellent insulation.

In these countries, the roofing material too is likely to have been gathered locally. The earliest and most easily available solutions such as thatch were often unsatisfactory in areas where they could never properly dry out. Thus at the time that walls were beginning to be built of permanent materials, so too were roofs. Clay could be baked into roof tiles of different shapes, and once the roofs of London were covered with them. From the end of the eighteenth century they were increasingly replaced by slate from Wales or the north-west and south-west of England – a hard, thin material that easily provided a waterproof layer. In fact slate was also often used to provide a damp-proof course before the invention of more modern materials and methods.

must know
Pantiles
Pantiles are clay roof tiles with a section in the form of a flat S shape. When laid they create a characteristic wavy surface, and in seaside areas one can sometimes see them glazed in cheerful colours. Unlike plain tiles, they overlap horizontally as well as vertically, providing effective protection.

The primary function of the roof is to keep rain out of the house, and to throw it away from the walls.

Materials and architecture

You know that the materials houses are made from are usually derived from the area they are built in. That is the first stage in understanding the logic of architectural tradition and style.

Brickwork in England is traditionally laid in either English bond (top) or Flemish bond (bottom).

Structure and decoration

It is a natural characteristic of mankind to try to impose both order and decoration onto created objects. It is also natural for anyone who works with their hands continually to want to improve and refine the work they are doing. It is because of this that the basic materials and methods of building have evolved all over the world into sophisticated architectural styles.

Simply using the materials to hand in the method best suited for working with them will always provide a certain consistency. With that consistency comes a logical degree of natural variation. Bricks can be made in different colours and with different textures, for example. Some stone, such as the flint found around the south and east of England, is naturally varied in appearance, and it can be cut in different ways or mixed with brick. And clay tiles moulded into different patterns can be used to clad walls. All these add variety to the local architecture of a place without in any way disturbing its consistent character.

Brick bonds

If your house is built of brick, have a look to see how the bricks are laid. In most modern buildings, they are simply laid end to end longways: that is because they are simply forming a skin over the rest of the building structure within. But traditionally they were laid in different ways to ensure a strong bond across a thick wall.

The most common bond is the Flemish bond, in which you can see the long and short ends of the brick (known respectively as the stretchers and the headers) alternately along a single course. An alternative is English bond, which was often used in mediaeval times and was revived by the Victorians: here you will see an entire course of headers followed above by an entire course of stretchers. Some of the bricks could be of a different colour. With possibilities like these, it is easy to create attractive, but logical, variations in the character of different walls in one region.

Adding features

Walls and roofs are important, but they are of course not the only major features of a building. The other basic elements of a building are described below in the order in which they developed historically.

Chimneys

At first, fires were simply lit in the middle of a room, and the smoke went out through a hole in the ceiling. In time permanent fireplaces were built. In country areas you can sometimes see where a brick chimney was added to an older timber-framed house. By placing a pair of fireplaces back to back within a house, it was possible to have two fireplaces using the same chimney stack. The fireplaces of another pair of rooms on an upper floor could later be incorporated economically. In time, builders and architects could begin to use the

Some of the great houses of the Tudor era have magnificent brick chimneys such as these.

prominent form of the chimney as a major element in their design of a house.

The tops of the chimneys could become decorative objects in their own right. Builders of large houses in Tudor times created some beautiful ornamental chimneys.

Staircases

The obvious way of extending a house cheaply was to use the space up in the roof. In many old houses a floor was simply added in the middle of the space to create two low rooms, and the residents would have used a ladder to move between the two.

In time, however, the ladder developed into a permanent staircase. If there was a solid wall within the house, for example as part of the chimney construction, it could also support the stairs. When houses were built in rows, the staircase was generally located alongside the party wall with the neighbour, because it did not necessarily require natural light in the way that a room does. That may well explain the position of the staircase in your house.

A window on a gable shows that roof space has been exploited for an extra room.

Gables

Building tall roofs to throw off rain meant that there was potentially a great deal of space in the upper part of a house. Most simple houses had a gable at either end of the roof, but by building more of them the owners could increase the headroom in the attic and gain another valuable bedroom. You can look out for this in old buildings that have been added to over the years.

People found gables attractive in their own right, because they gave another opportunity for variety that made sense economically. They also provided more space on the outside of the building for decoration. For some, the distinct shape of a tall gable came to represent their idea of what a home ought to look like. That is why many modern buildings have gables on them, even where they are not perhaps strictly necessary.

The gable is a familiar symbol of a home, and thus popular with developers.

Doors, windows and joinery

We have looked at the massive elements of buildings that give them their basic character. Now it is time to look at those important details of a building which provide a key to developing architectural traditions.

Getting in and seeing out

The parts of the building we have looked at so far are permanent and fixed: they were intended by those that created them to remain where they were for hundreds of years. But many other elements of buildings are intended to be flexible in some way. In particular, doors and windows need to open and close. And because they (unlike most parts of the building) are in regular daily use by the occupants, they need to have special characteristics to make them easily identifiable and pleasant to use.

Until very recent times, all doors were made of timber, and both doors and windows had timber frames. Timber is easily worked by hand, and over generations joiners began to perfect the details of their designs. If you look at unaltered older buildings in any one particular area you will see that they largely share the same characteristics. In a Victorian street, for example, you will notice that front doors are similar, and windows are made so that they open in the same way. The ironmongery may be the same from house to house, too. To some extent that is because it was more economical for a builder to use the same pattern over and over again; indeed, identifying common details like this can tell us which houses were built by which builders. But it is just as true that architects and builders felt that these details provided an opportunity for a house to show that it belonged to a family of houses of the same type, which may have been a way of demonstrating the status of a speculative building development to potential customers.

Houses in a Georgian terrace, for example, may share common details such as fanlights and wrought-iron balconies. Anyone approaching them would be able to guess what kind of house they were entering. The quality of the decorative plasterwork inside would also tell visitors about the type of place they were in.

The double-hung vertical sliding sash is an English invention. Counterweights attached to cords can hold the window open in any position.

Casement windows with leaded lights give a feeling of domesticity and comfort.

Timber details

By inspecting the timber details of a house it is possible to get as good an idea of the style of a building as it is by looking at the major features such as the walls and chimneys.

- solid, plain oak door and window frames with squared edges and simple joints are either very old, or are conscious imitations of mediaeval work.
- painted broad sections of timber, often with simple curved edges, are characteristic of seventeenth-century joinery.
- complex painted sections of timber, sometimes made up by pinning several strips over each other,

became common from the late seventeenth century onwards. This type of joinery makes a great deal of use of 'ogee' mouldings – strips of timber that are cut into the form of an S.

• varnished or polished (rather than painted) timber became fashionable in early Victorian times. Over the nineteenth century, the standard of joinery

The front door is an important place to make a statement. It may be the only decorative feature on the street front of a house.

became highly sophisticated. Some late Victorian architects were intrigued by the superb quality of Japanese joinery, and tried to imitate it where their budget would allow it.

• plain, minimal timber or metal sections, usually painted, became common for most housing from the 1930s onwards. The reason was not only economy: it was also because architectural fashion was reacting against the complexity of earlier styles.

Wrought iron balconies and verandahs became popular during the Regency era.

The design of other timber parts of the house developed in the same way. Eighteenth- and nineteenth-century skirting boards in a large house, for example, were characteristically tall and ornamental, whereas more modern houses have very minimal ones. Their purpose is to mask the join between the plastered wall and the floor.

More about doors and windows

Doors and windows do more than simply function: they also add important interest. Those who design and build houses are always looking out for ways in which they can give a place a special dignity and significance without wasting money. The arrangement and style of the openings is a logical way to do this.

It does not seem to be the case that rooms were historically designed to suit a certain layout of furniture, because up to the end of the eighteenth century most people had very little in the way of moveable belongings. Rooms were seen primarily as flexible open spaces, and were much more important than anything within them. Special attention was therefore given to the position of the door and windows.

must know
Dormer windows
Dormer windows are windows that project from the roof. Sometimes the front face of the window lines up with the front face of the wall below: this is called a lucarne window. The other common type of dormer sits further up on the roof, detached from the wall below. The French call this a *chien assis* window - a 'sitting dog'!

The door to a room in an eighteenth-century stately home: decorative joinery at its most magnificent.

must know

More about windows

The position and shape of windows have a great effect on the appearance of a house. A bay window that provides light for most of the day as the sun moves around it can be a very distinctive feature. And the arrangement of large and small windows in any house gives a clue as to where the important rooms are on the inside, which in turn adds the kind of logical interest to a building that architects are always trying to achieve.

In some cases, the door might be in the middle of a room, facing the fireplace: in fact, a fireplace operates best when it is positioned directly opposite a door. This easily gives certain grandeur to any room. There was unlikely to be much choice as to the wall on which the windows would be positioned, but the architect could decide how many there would be, and what their proportions should be. If it was possible to match up the proportions between all the various different openings, so that for example the windows on the upper floors would be exactly three-quarters of the size of the ones downstairs, the result would be likely to look elegant and balanced.

Recording buildings

Buildings need to be recorded for several reasons. An original design must be drawn carefully so that it can be built accurately. But photographs of completed buildings are important too, to convey and explain the character and style of a house to others.

must know
Keeping historical records
Keeping an accurate record of our historical buildings is so important that the national public institutions of many countries invest a great deal of time and money in doing it properly. The 'Survey of London', for example, is a continuing series of detailed studies of the buildings of the capital that first appeared in 1900. It is now edited by historians at English Heritage.

Drawings

You may well have seen drawings that have been made so that builders can construct a house. It is important to bear in mind that these drawings are prepared using certain conventions. This is so that everyone knows what to expect, from the person who is paying for the house to the council official who will want to discuss a planning application. It is also, of course, so that those who work on a building site know exactly what they are supposed to do, and can calculate the costs in advance.

There has been little change in the way in which a building is presented on paper since the seventeenth century. To ensure that all the necessary information is understandable, it is always shown using the following three methods:

Plans

A plan is a drawing of the layout of the rooms of a building. There must always be a separate plan for each floor – by looking out for the position of the staircase which connects between them one can easily see how the plans fit 'on top of one another'. The plan will also show the doors and the windows, and all the built-in fitments such as wardrobes and (in a modern building) the kitchen and bathroom fittings. A plan is technically a downwards view of a horizontal slice through a building.

Sections

A section is a view of a vertical slice through a building. It is unlikely, of course, to show all the rooms, but it does clearly show many aspects which the plan cannot. It shows the height of the rooms, and therefore is the key to understanding how the staircase will look. It may also explain what the roof looks like, and how it stays up. If a building is making a feature of different room heights, a section may well be needed in order to explain what the effect will be.

Elevations

The elevations are views of the walls of a building. Some of the internal elevations will appear on the sections, but the external ones need to be drawn separately. Although the architect may draw these last, because they are dependent on the plans and sections, it is of course the exterior aspect that is

Plans, sections and elevations are indispensable tools when constructing or recording a building.

likely to interest other people most at first. A 'facade'
is another word for an elevation of an external wall,
but one that implies an elevation which is special or
more important.

Matching the plans, sections and elevations of the
same building requires going back and forward over
and over again to achieve a balanced design. People
who watch architects in restaurants are often
amused to see them doodling all over the paper
napkins – they seem obsessive scribblers. Now you
know what they are doing, and why!

Three-dimensional renderings

Architects have always tried to present their
buildings in the form of three-dimensional drawings,
and computer software now makes it easy to create
accurate views in and around buildings. It is not
unusual to see animated cartoon-like films that can
give a realistic impression of what walking through a
building will be like. Some architects actually use the
techniques of computer rendering to inspire their
designs for their buildings.

All drawings must be presented at a known scale –
that is, as a fixed miniaturized proportion of the real
thing – in order that dimensions can be checked
using a special ruler. Now that nearly all drawings are
done using computers, the architect actually draws
at full size, which of course is reduced for
convenience on the computer monitor itself; and
printouts can easily be made at any scale at the press
of the button.

All contemporary homes are extremely
complicated objects. In order to record your own

home thoroughly enough to rebuild it from scratch, you would need a whole series of drawings beyond the basic ones listed here. At the least you would need separate drawings for the electrical layout, the plumbing and the drainage, and the landscaping of the area outside; and you would probably also require detailed drawings at a large scale in order to convey sufficient information about the joinery and other internal fittings. It can readily be appreciated that the ability to draw accurately is an invaluable part of the architectural profession, and becoming familiar with architectural drawings will be an important part of your discovery of architectural history.

Photographs

While a scale drawing is an invaluable tool, there are plenty of other ways of conveying what a building is really like. The most obvious one of all is clear from the pages of this book: photography.

A photograph, unlike a scale drawing, is not usually intended to provide an objective description of a building. More probably, it is there to show its character, and to emphasize what makes it special. Photography can highlight certain features, and of course it can enhance colours and contrasts. It is also a useful tool for pointing out common features between buildings, either by capturing a view of several buildings at once or by focusing on particular elements.

Both perspective drawing and photography are invaluable tools in recording architecture. Developing a skill at one of these is highly recommended for anyone who wants to analyse and discuss buildings.

must know
Plans and planning
Anyone submitting an application for planning permission must submit plans, sections and elevations. As a result, your local town hall will have a substantial archive of drawings which can be consulted by any member of the public.

Architectural style

There is another important way of recording architecture: writing about it. The history of style brings together all the different aspects of what a building looks and feels like as a continuous story. That is what the rest of this book is mainly about.

must know
Architectural style and the cinema
Architectural style is not only for real buildings. Some architects have designed sets for theatrical productions, and in the early days of the cinema there were a few whose ideas proved influential. Occasionally this influence travels the other way. Ridley Scott's *Blade Runner* (1982), and Tim Burton's *Batman* (1989), which won an Oscar for designers Anton Furst and Peter Young, had considerable impact on architectural style.

Style

It is possible that you can now begin to compare the house you live in with others that you know: you already have a sense of what the important elements are. And yet we have not yet looked at the idea of architectural style.

All civilizations see themselves as part of an unfolding history. Ours is no different. We characterize past generations by remembering important dates and events, and associating them with changes that have come over society. The more people learn about the world, the more they want to express their own judgement about what seems important, and what lessons are worth remembering and repeating.

Architecture is like that. From time immemorial people have built using the materials that have come to hand. At certain times in history, structures have been erected in different places in the world that have seemed unforgettable: indeed, the more one looks at them, the more they seem to offer. Some ideas have been copied directly and others have been adapted. Many have come to be taken for granted. But in all cases it is the notion of style – of the common visual language of buildings of a certain type – that provides the key to understanding where these ideas have come from.

Where our history begins

This history of architecture starts with the temples of ancient Greece, a civilization that had already lost its dominance two thousand years ago. The reason why these buildings are worth remembering can easily be learned by a trip to any historic town centre. There will certainly be buildings there, some constructed comparatively recently, that display characteristic Greek detailing; and there may be some that try on a tiny scale to imitate parts of a Greek temple. In order to understand why this might be, it is important to learn what Greek architecture had to offer, and to see how it fits into a long, continuing story.

At just the time when a Greek-style bank was being built in one part of your town, a gothic-style church might have been going up in another. The first building would have evoked feelings of solidity and responsibility; the second, an attempt to reconnect with the spirituality of the Middle Ages. Architects, and the people they build for, have always known that the style of a building carries certain associations. At the same time, they cannot usually go right back to imitate precisely a building from the distant past, because practical needs have changed. So the story of architecture is one in which designers are continually looking at ideas from the past and updating them in order to come up with something suitable. It is this that makes the story of architecture so dynamic and so exciting.

Your house and style

It may well be that at first glance your own home does not appear to occupy a distinguished position in the history of style and of past civilizations.

But that is unlikely to be true. Your house, whenever it was built, can tell you a great deal, and all you need to do is to learn to read it.

Looking for common features between your building and its neighbours is a good place to start. If you look at detailed maps in your local history library, you can probably work out when your house was built, and which other ones were built at the same time. Sometimes one can clearly see that a whole field, or the garden of a large house, was all built on at once.

Having done that, you can look for common features between your house and your neighbours' – or others in the same area. Blocks of flats that were all built by a local authority during the same decade will probably have as much in common as houses built in a street by the same Georgian or Victorian builder. It will not take long for you to be able to

must know
The style of your house
Most buildings in any country are private homes, and the reasons for building houses have never really changed: a sturdily-built home is generally an excellent investment for the builder or buyer. One way, therefore, of distinguishing between homes of different periods is to concentrate on differences of style. In England, the developers of the Georgian era chose a neat and regular style which recalled for them the dignity of Roman architecture, whereas the house builders of the 1930s preferred a 'Tudor' look which suggested warmth, solidity and comfort.

identify which materials are the same, and whether
they are characteristic of the area as a whole. You
can make a list of all the features in your house
which belong to the period in which it was built – you
may have to pop into a neighbour's house in order to
be sure which ones are original if you think some
have been changed.

Knowing when your house was built means that
you can distinguish it from others in your town, and
also what links it with other houses built at the same
time. And this is where the story of architecture that
follows will start to make sense. You will find to your
surprise that although you live neither in a Greek
temple nor a gothic cathedral, you can very probably
identify common ideas with both.

Making historical references

In the seventeenth and eighteenth centuries, builders
would commonly copy the features of ancient Greek
or Roman buildings onto anything larger than a
medium-sized house. They would imitate the
grandness of these ancient structures by ensuring

that the new house was symmetrical, with a door in the middle of the front elevation. They would give that door special importance by putting a miniature temple pediment over it. They would copy the stone mouldings from famous buildings that they knew or had heard of, and use them to decorate the corners and openings of their own construction. Architects who took a particular interest in the civilizations of the past, and who longed for order and elegance in modern times, might apply Greek columns to the front of a house, or even a Roman dome to the top of it. The result would never have been mistaken for a genuine temple, and yet at the time the references to classical antiquity are unmistakeable.

You do not have to live in an eighteenth-century Roman-style house, or a nineteenth-century gothic-style one, to be able to find references to the past. Many small terraced houses have tiny details around the front door or windows which were enough to add dignity to their otherwise economical form. Many mid-twentieth-century blocks of flats were designed by people who valued very highly classical ideas of proportion and who consequently put great store by the shapes of windows, or the overall forms of the blocks they designed. Others saw modern building necessities as a way of recalling the gothic principle of expressing function. A large chimney or a prominent balcony could easily be the modern descendants of a mediaeval manor house – improbable though that may at first seem.

Architecture and history

On top of all this, all buildings are part of the broader history of any nation. Building a new house is such

Designers in the arts and crafts era of the late nineteenth and early twentieth centuries were inspired by the solid workmanship of mediaeval times.

an expensive project that it inevitably involves many, many people: not only those who will pay for it (which may include a bank rather than an individual!) but also those who will be involved in building it. That means that the final structure is in some way inevitably representative of the society in which it was built. That is one of many reasons why the history of architecture is so fascinating a subject.

want to know more?

Take it to the next level...
- Families of design, 42
- Architecture and personality, 170
- Getting a clear idea of a new building, 186

Other sources...
- Making an accurate drawing using a scale ruler of part of your own home will teach you more than you expected about how it was designed. Make a plan and elevation of one of the rooms, and use it to experiment with furniture and picture arrangements. It is a useful exercise that will impress on you the value of scale drawing.
- It is also a surprisingly useful exercise to try to describe a building you know well accurately enough for a friend to make a sketch of it from your words alone. Try to be as exact as you can with the height, width, and position and shape of the windows, and see what happens. Looking at buildings accurately enough to be able to remember them well is an invaluable skill.

Further reading

Adolph, Anthony, *Collins Tracing Your Home's History* (Collins, 2006)
Brunskill, R.W., *Vernacular Architecture: an Illustrated Handbook* (Faber & Faber, new edition 2000)
Clifton-Taylor, Alec, *The Pattern of English Building* (Faber & Faber, 1972)
Thom, Colin, *Researching London's Houses* (Historical Publications, 2005)

2 The classical tradition

We have discovered that many design aspects of architecture, from the general form to the smallest details, can easily be found in buildings of different types and different historical periods. That is because builders and designers choose to work within a particular design tradition. Distinguishing between these traditions is one of the most important elements when learning how to read a building. We start with the classical tradition, possibly the most prominent feature of western architecture.

Families of design

The simplest way of approaching all design traditions is to think of each one as a family. The members of a family have similar, but not identical traits. Getting to know one member of the family well provides an excellent introduction to their 'relatives'.

must know
People and buildings
Leonardo da Vinci was one of several famous designers and thinkers in history who created a direct parallel between human beings and the form of a building. Several architects in renaissance Italy drew plans of buildings and geometrical shapes with outlines of men superimposed over them.

Meeting the family

A family member might be a whole building, a type of layout or plan, or even just a small piece of an overall design. If, for example, the general form of a building such as a nineteenth-century town hall belongs to the classical family, you will expect that the features inside and out – the windows, the cornices, even the door handles – will all be classical too, or at least will relate to each other in some way.

You can thus easily appreciate that it is possible to think of whole buildings as being senior members of a family, and of the details as being junior relations. One might even say that some of the most influential buildings in history have been the 'grandparents' of a smaller building, such as our town hall for example.

As with all families, there are misfits and there are eccentrics. There are family members that stand out, and there are others that are more reclusive. There might be an aunt hidden away in the countryside somewhere, or a successful nephew in town. The analogy is not far fetched: you will discover that the characteristics of architecture have personalities, and influences. Some are more welcome than others; and many take getting to know well before you can understand where they have come from.

When architects throughout history have approached a new design, they have usually looked at one of the traditional families for inspiration, and then put together a building that incorporates all the different elements from it at varying scales and in different ways – rather as if you had invited a particular group of family members to a party. In this way, the design will seem coherent and familiar. Yet at the same time the resulting building offers many opportunities for the architect to demonstrate their personal discretion, because different designers will put similar elements together in different ways.

If you keep an eye out when visiting the centres of different towns, you will notice that some of the older banks or chains of shops will have similar, but slightly different, buildings in each high street. That way, the branch will be familiar to their customers, and yet still slightly different from place to place. Devising buildings that are both familiar and yet different, coherent and yet varied, has long been one of the central aims of architects.

This and the following chapter will introduce you to the two leading families of architecture: the classical, and the gothic. Each of them has its ancestors and its wilful youngsters. To some extent they have 'intermarried' – for at different times architects have chosen to blend elements from each of the two styles to create unique buildings for special situations.

When you meet the leading members of these families face to face – that is, you visit the great historical masterpieces of architecture – you may be surprised and delighted by what you see. You will discover too that the ideas behind these buildings are often as intriguing as their appearance.

Ancient Greece

The most prominent family in architecture is the classical tradition. This began with a series of buildings in Ancient Greece, mainly during the first millennium BC, which has continued to inspire architects on and off ever since.

must know
Discovering Ancient Greece
The masterpieces of ancient Greek architecture were not appreciated in the West until two English architects and painters, James Stuart and Nicholas Revett, started preparing their massive illustrated book *The Antiquities of Athens* in the mid-eighteenth century. The work was published in several volumes between 1762 and 1816.

The great Greek temples

There are a number of buildings in ancient Greek civilization which truly are the grandparents of the classical tradition. Striking when first built, rediscovered (and sometimes reconstructed) throughout history, and endlessly copied on a large and small scale all over the western world right up to the present day, these great monuments provide the first lesson in architectural language.

In the middle of the fifth century BC the Athenian ruler Pericles built the Parthenon, a temple to the goddess Athena, on the rocky outcrop called the Acropolis beside the city. In many respects this building has come to represent the finest Greek architecture of the period.

Identifying the Greek temple

A chamber with a colonnade

The Parthenon consisted of two rectangular inner chambers surrounded on all four sides by a colonnade. The temple originally had a low pitched roof.

A temple front with a pediment

The roof was supported at the two narrow ends of the temple by triangular stone gables known as pediments.

It is the resulting appearance of these narrow ends that more than anything characterizes the Greek temple.

The Parthenon was not the first temple like this, and nor was it the biggest, but because of its location it was possibly the most striking. In addition, the Parthenon provides a demonstration both of a distinctive overall form but also of the way in which all the details add up to create a coherent and adaptable architectural style.

The style of the columns

The columns of the Parthenon are plain and substantial. They sit directly, without any ornamental base, on the platform on which the temple stands. At the top they have 'heads' in the form of a stone cushion topped by a rectangular block.

The architrave and the frieze

The columns support a continuous line of stone lintels (called an architrave), and above that is a frieze which is decorated at regular intervals by vertical strips (called triglyphs). Then the pediment itself tops the structure along the narrow ends of the building.

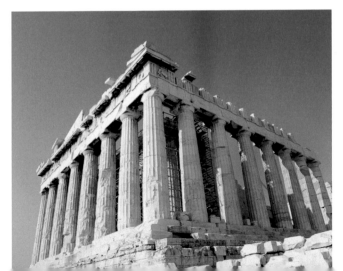

The Parthenon in Athens, designed in the Doric order, is often considered to be the masterpiece of ancient Greek architecture.

Birmingham Town Hall was designed in the 1830s by Joseph Hansom, who was clearly inspired by ancient Greek temples.

The orders of Greek architecture

Greek architecture is primarily distinguished by the bold external form of its temples. There is however a second basic element: the decorative style of the columns, the architrave and the frieze. The combination used at the Parthenon is called the Doric order.

All these design features – and many more that can be found on the building – have specific terms. There are two other Greek orders. You can distinguish between them right away by looking at the capitals – the proper name for the stone tops of the columns – and very soon you will notice that each order has a different group of details that goes with it as well. All these details were originally painted with contrasting colours to make them stand out.

The Ionic order

Soon after the Parthenon was completed, a shrine was built alongside the Parthenon called the Erechtheion. The capitals of the columns have ear-like projections – called volutes – and these are the most distinctive feature of the Ionic order. Ionic

The Doric column has a simple capital that resembles a cushion of stone.

columns sit on elegant bases. The carving of the decoration around the frieze in Ionic buildings was generally much more delicate and varied than on Doric ones.

The Corinthian order

As the Parthenon was being built, a third major order developed. This is the Corinthian order, and you can again recognize it by the design of the capitals at the top of the columns. This time they have been carved with leaves – actually, with a representation of the leaf of the acanthus plant.

The details of the rest of the buildings constructed in the Corinthian order were often refined further than they were in the Ionic, and in fact two of the most famous ancient buildings in the style are comparatively small and delicate structures: a monument to Lysicrates, built in Athens in 334 BC, and a little octagonal structure called the Tower of the Winds, built in the city as a sundial around the middle of the first century BC.

must know
Four great Ionic buildings
• The Erechtheion, Athens (c 421-405 BC)
• The Temple of Nikè Apteros, Athens (c 448-421 BC)
• The Nereid Monument, Xanthos (c 400 BC; the remains are in the British Museum)
• The Temple of Athena Polias at Priene (begun c 340 BC)

The most distinctive features of the Ionic order are the curved projections on the capitals, called volutes.

must know

Four masterpieces of the Corinthian order

• The temple of Olympian Zeus at Athens (174 BC–AD 132)
• The Choragic Monument of Lysicrates, Athens (334 BC)
• The Tower of the Winds, Athens (mid-first century BC)
• The interior of the Temple of Apollo Epicurius, Bassae (c 429–400 BC)

Why Greek architecture is important

Ancient Greek civilization has provided posterity with many memorable buildings, some of which still stand: indeed, one might well say that the fine quality of Greek architecture was one of the reasons why Greek civilization as a whole has been so important to posterity. It showed that in refining different groups of details, and using different orders for different purposes, it was possible to build consistently but without becoming repetitive.

It is easy to appreciate that perhaps the leading characteristic of Greek architecture was the importance it gave to the columns, capitals and

The Erechtheion, the Parthenon's Ionic neighbour, is famous also for its caryatids, or columns modelled on the female body.

beams. Because upright and horizontal elements are so basic a part of most buildings for structural reasons, and because Greek builders clearly devoted a great deal of their attention to getting the proportions and the details of these features exactly right, these early temples have established for many people the basic rules of architecture.

Furthermore, by varying the proportions and the details of the orders, Greek temples have much in common with each other, but they are never identical. At different times over history, architects and critics have devoted themselves to tracing the exact

The decoration on Corinthian capitals is based on acanthus leaves. The fillets cut into the shafts of the columns are called flutes.

must know

**Later
interpretations of
the Greek temple**

In the nineteenth
century, several
architects designed
buildings directly
modelled on the
Corinthian temple.
These include the Town
Hall, Birmingham, and
St George's Hall,
Liverpool, in England;
the Madeleine church in
Paris, and the National
Gallery in Berlin.

appearance of all the features of the orders, and to watching the ways in which they were varied over time and across the areas of the eastern Mediterranean and Aegean that the Greeks controlled.

Vitruvius, a Roman architect, described the stocky Doric column as representing a man; the elegant Ionic order as representing a mature woman; and the Corinthian as being symbolic of a young girl. So the members of this first branch of the classical family have been associated with human beings right from the start.

The distinctive appearance of the Greek temple, with its columns and pediments, has come to represent this type of architecture as a whole.

The delightful Tower of the Winds in Athens, built in the first century BC, is delicate as well as powerful.

When you see any building, anywhere, with a 'temple front' you can be sure that it is intended to be reminiscent of the Greek classical family of architecture.

Earlier civilizations

The Greeks were not the first to develop a coherent type of building style, even if their buildings were the most refined of the early European civilizations. The Egyptians built the great pyramids at Giza, directly south of modern Cairo, in the middle of the third millennium BC. These pyramids were burial chambers where rulers and their queens were laid to rest with their treasures; the Great Pyramid of King Cheops (built over a period of about 75 years around 2500 BC) has a base that measures over 230 m (756 ft) along each side. A much later, partially surviving, building from the same civilization, and also a huge one, is the Temple of Amon-Re at Karnak (built by 1300 BC). This building is famous for having what seems like an entire forest of massive columns in one of its halls. These columns have decorated capitals which some think resemble palm leaves; but none of the surviving Egyptian structures seem to have the sophistication of the Greek ones, and fewer of them have been discovered.

Several other ancient middle-eastern civilizations built vast structures, too. King Nebuchadnezzar II of Babylon built 'The Hanging Gardens of Babylon' – in its day one of the wonders of the world, but sadly nothing is known now of its appearance. In the Pergamon Museum in Berlin, however, you can see his Ishtar Gate (605–563 BC), covered in glazed blue bricks and decorated with lions.

must know
More terminology from classical architecture
• entasis – the swelling around the centre of a column to make it appear robust
• metope – a plain or sculptural panel placed in the frieze. The 'Elgin Marbles' in London include the metopes of the Parthenon
• dentils – continuous teeth-like projections along an Ionic frieze
• architrave – the stone lintel that connects columns

Roman architecture

The architecture of the Romans was derived from that of the Greeks, but was much more varied due to improved building technology. Arches, for example, were invented and used for viaducts as well as colonnades. The many surviving examples of Roman architecture have inspired countless builders.

Adapting from Greece

The international dominance of the Romans in southern Europe followed that of the Greeks, and it was natural that the buildings of the new kingdom – and later, empire – should imitate their grandeur and delicacy. The Romans, however, adapted the rules they had learnt about architecture from the Greeks into a much wider range of constructional and decorative features. Like the Greek temple front, some of their inventions have come to define their architecture and can be recognized on buildings everywhere.

Two new orders

The Romans invented two further orders: the Tuscan, with its simple, slender columns; and the Composite, which looks like a combination of the Corinthian and the Ionic.

New building types

They also used adapted architectural features for use on many different types of buildings, including bath houses, markets, commemorative arches and even huge structures for games (such as the Colosseum in Rome, which was built towards the end of the first century AD for gladiatorial combat). The Romans also built aqueducts and bridges, such as the spectacular Pont du Gard at Nîmes in the south of France. In addition, their houses – often in the form of low buildings grouped around open courts – have survived across Europe; in the town of Pompeii, buried when the volcano Vesuvius erupted in AD 79, whole homes and their decorations have survived comparatively intact up to the present day.

The fourth-century arch of Constantine in Rome demonstrates how the Romans combined the orders with new curved forms.

must know
The Roman forum
The forum of a Roman city was the central open space and used for markets, meeting places and demonstrations. The forum in Rome, which has been partly uncovered by excavation, consisted of a series of fine temples surrounded by porticos and decorated with statues and monuments.

New structural forms

Probably the most significant characteristic of the Romans, however, was the frequent use of the semi-circular arch, and of the stone vaulted roof. They discovered that stones built into the form of an arch will be self supporting, each one being held in place by the one either side. Using these, they were able to span large distances between columns – something the Greeks had never been able to do.

At the Pont du Gard in the south of France, Roman engineers combined modern technology with architectural elegance.

They achieved this also because of the invention and development of new materials such as a light concrete. The most astounding achievement in this respect was a vast temple called the Pantheon, which was built in Rome in the second century AD and still stands today. One huge hemispherical masonry dome – with a diameter of just over 43 m (over 142 ft) – covers the whole of the interior of the building.

The Pantheon was erected for the Emperor Hadrian at the beginning of the second century AD, and has survived magnificently.

must know
Roman temples
The Romans built temples to match those of the Greeks. The 'Maison Carrée' in Nîmes, France, is a spectacular Corinthian temple, while the Temple of Vesta at Tivoli outside Rome is a picturesque round building.

Classical architecture reborn

Roman architecture lasted as long as the Roman Empire itself – until the middle of the fourth century AD. Soon after, their great structures began to fall into ruins, and were pillaged for the building materials by disparate tribes. So how and where did its influence survive?

must know
Vitruvius
Vitruvius' great work on architecture is called *De Architectura*, or 'On Architecture'. It survived in manuscript form throughout the Middle Ages, but achieved immortality when it was first printed in the late fifteenth century. Various Italian editions followed, but an English translation did not appear for almost 200 years.

The Italian renaissance

The centuries between the collapse of the Roman Empire and its rediscovery in the fifteenth century saw the invention and growth of the second great family: the gothic tradition. And yet nevertheless, the Greek and especially the Roman styles have been rediscovered several times throughout history, often becoming once again the dominant way of building.

The first significant revival of the Roman way of building came with the Italian renaissance in the fifteenth century, and in particular around the sophisticated, culturally rich areas of Rome and Tuscany. The designers of the age, in common with everyone else, lived in towns built on the half-submerged ruins of the Roman Empire, and in time they began to see themselves as the inheritors of a great tradition common to all Italians across the fragmented peninsular. Furthermore, by the end of the century, architects and their clients had access to new printed editions of a book written during the reign of the Emperor Augustus by a Roman architect called Marcus Vitruvius Pollo. Vitruvius had not as far as we know been a great designer himself, but his book described in detail the way

The Foundlings' Hospital in Florence, designed by Brunelleschi in 1419, is usually considered to be the first building of the renaissance.

the Romans had built; and he also defined the role and duties of an architect as an independent professional acting for a client.

The renaissance is often said to begin with the buildings designed in Florence by Filippo Brunelleschi. Brunelleschi had trained as a sculptor, and it was perhaps because of his well-developed sense of three-dimensional space, together with his interest in Roman structures, that he came to solve the problem of how to build a great dome over the cathedral in Florence (1420–36). He had earlier designed a building in the city called the Foundlings' Hospital (1419), which used arcades of Corinthian columns and Roman details such as pediments. It is sometimes thought of as the first building of the renaissance.

From that point on, adaptations and variations of Roman buildings increasingly became the dominant style for prestigious and public buildings: firstly across Italy; then throughout Europe; and then, over time, in most of the lands across the world that were

must know
Brunelleschi
Brunelleschi was the first architect of the renaissance, but his fame is also due to his success in building a massive masonry dome over the cathedral in Florence – a challenge that had defeated other architects. His solution used brickwork laid in a herringbone pattern and tied with iron rings and chains.

must know
Florence
The powerful
mercantile city of
Florence saw the first
flowering of
renaissance
architecture. Other
important buildings of
the period include the
church of Santo Spirito,
and the Pazzi chapel,
both probably designed
by Brunelleschi himself.

colonized by the West. This reinvented classical architecture is called neo-classical architecture.

Why should Roman architecture be revived?

It is important to grasp the reasons for wanting to revive the Roman style, because they tell us a great deal about why architecture is important at all: important to particular builders, important to all the arts, and important to the whole of society and culture.

In spite of Brunelleschi's remarkable buildings, a revived style did not suddenly land in Florence at once. Architects slowly began to recognize the different features of the ancient buildings they had inherited, and to experiment with similar ideas themselves. Leon Battista Alberti, who is considered like Brunelleschi to be one of the fathers of renaissance architecture, designed alterations to existing gothic buildings in a classical style. At the church of Santa Maria Novella in Florence (1456–70), for example, he designed a Roman-type front as a kind of screen to a gothic church behind. He also wrote a highly influential treatise, called *On the Art of Building*, which was probably a conscious attempt at imitating the great work of Vitruvius, and which also explained the relevance of Roman design to modern building.

One argument for reviving Roman architecture was that the Roman period, especially the time of Augustus, was associated with an educated, comfortable lifestyle and a prosperous, civilizing empire. But in fact the implications go much further than that. Up to the time of Brunelleschi and Alberti, architecture had been in a state of continuous change, which also meant that it was different wherever one went because of local conditions and materials. The idea of plunging into a distant era and retrieving the building of a past time was revolutionary. It implied that there were certain basic truths in life which the ancient peoples had appreciated, and which had been lost or confused in modern times.

The idea of the classical family can illustrate this again. Imagine hearing of long-lost relatives who had performed great deeds, and then making the effort slowly but surely of getting in touch with them again. A distinguished old grandparent may in the meantime have lost an eye or a leg, but he or she is still something of an old warrior and, with excitement but also by experiment, you can dedicate yourself to making up for what is missing. That is what the renaissance architects seem to have been doing. And of course in so doing, they got to know themselves a great deal better and began to develop in different ways as designers.

Bramante's delightful design for a small chapel in Rome, called the Tempietto San Pietro, is a graceful reinterpretation of Roman architecture.

Neo-classical architecture

Neo-classical architecture is not just about rediscovering the past: it is also about developing and experimenting with it. Revived Roman architecture provided Italian designers with wonderful opportunities for playing with the rules and inventing new forms.

The developing classical revival

Renaissance designers realized that Roman architects had gone a great deal further than the Greeks because of the way in which they had been prepared to experiment with columns and beams, and to integrate them with new structural achievements.

Looking back at Italian neo-classical architecture, we can identify certain important new elements that were added to the Roman canon.

The Palladian house

From the mid-1540s onwards the Italian architect Andrea Palladio built a series of houses on the mainland near Venice that were highly influential. Most of them combine an ornate temple-type front with a satisfyingly geometrical modern home behind. Palladio wrote about and published illustrations of his own designs, with the result that they were well known throughout Europe.

The colonnade

Many designers of the renaissance and the later stages of the classical revival developed ingenious and original ways of designing columned fronts for their buildings. A beautiful example is the little round church of 1502–10 dedicated to San Pietro in Rome, by Donato Bramante.

must know
Palladio
Andrea Palladio's *Four Books on Architecture* were published in 1570, and brought his villa designs to a wide audience. Among the motifs associated with his work is the tripartite 'Palladian' (or 'Venetian') window, which is an arched window set immediately between two flat-topped ones. He also designed the church of San Georgio Maggiore in Venice (1564-80).

The classical church front

Because there were no surviving Roman churches, classical architects had to invent a way of combining the 'pagan' architecture of the past with the traditional layout of a building that has a nave and aisles designed for Christian worship. Results can be seen all over Italy, including such masterpieces as Brunelleschi's Santo Spirito in Florence (from 1436), Alberti's San Andrea, Mantua (begun 1470), and – the biggest of them all – St Peter's, Rome. The seat of the pope was designed over a period of more than 100 years (from 1506) by a succession of some of the greatest architects of the period, including Bramante and Michelangelo.

The arched window

There had been monumental arches in ancient Roman architecture, but renaissance architects miniaturized them to create delicate windows of different sizes. At the library of San Marco in Venice, Jacopo Sansovino combined these with a colonnade to create a distinctively renaissance type of building in the mid-sixteenth century.

Palladio's Villa Capra, built near Vicenza from the 1560s, was designed as a country retreat and has inspired architects ever since.

The spread of neo-classicism

Neo-classical design came to dominate western architecture for over 200 years, and architects continued to invent and develop new forms for different types of buildings.

must know
Four breathtaking Italian baroque interiors
• San Carlo alle Quattro Fontane, Rome (Borromini, from 1637)
• San Ivo della Sapienza, Rome (Borromini, 1642–60)
• The Scala Regia at the Vatican (Bernini, 1663–6)
• The Capella della SS Sindone, Turin cathedral (Guarini, 1667–90)

Adaptability and personality

Architects had realized from the rediscovery of Roman architecture that the rules of classical architecture were infinitely variable, and allowed creative thinkers to experiment both with the facades of buildings and with the shapes of the spaces inside. As a result, the renaissance was followed by a series of phases which generated their own distinctive features.

The two most distinctive of these phases are called the 'mannerist' and the 'baroque'. Mannerist architects would typically mix together features from different orders, as well as inventing some of their own, to produce buildings that seemed to break the rules of design. Baroque architects, who dominated progressive European design for about a century from the early 1600s onwards, were distinguished by their rich three-dimensional treatment of space.

Whereas earlier neo-classical architects had tried to maintain clear and simple internal spaces, baroque designers such as Giovanni Bernini in Rome, Louis Le Vau in Paris, and Christopher Wren in London experimented with creating rooms that flow into one another, columns and cornices that seem to bend around the walls, and indirect light sources that add to the mystery of a place. These buildings were perhaps associated with Catholic

churches and the palaces of autocratic monarchs
(such as Versailles outside Paris) and as a result
there are comparatively few of them in the
predominantly Protestant north of Europe or the
United States.

The baroque style was not just limited to buildings.
Some of the most remarkable structures of its later
period form part of great landscaped ensembles.
Wren's Royal Naval Hospital at Greenwich (mainly
1699–1712), the gardens by André Le Nôtre at
Versailles (1661–87), and the house and park at
Chatsworth, Derbyshire (1684–1707) are all
magnificent examples of this approach.

The dome

Like Brunelleschi beforehand, Francesco Borromini
had been a sculptor before he became an architect
and he designed domes with dizzying internal
spaces. One of the best-known is that at San Carlo
alle Quattro Fontane in Rome (1637–41 and 1665–7).
Wren's dome at St Paul's is simpler than this one,
but it is a great deal bigger, and it is more illusionistic
than it first appears. Is it the descendant of
Bramante's little dome at San Pietro in Rome?

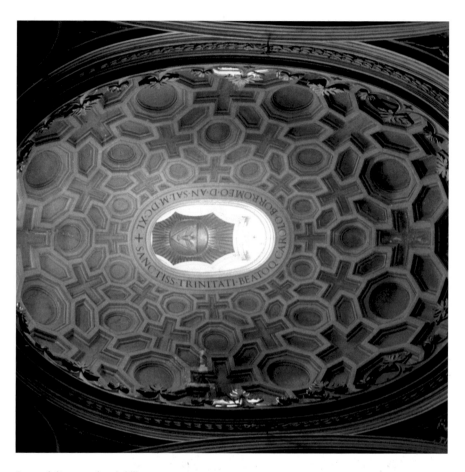

Borromini's exceptional skill at modelling three-dimensional space is demonstrated by the dome of San Carlo alle Quattro Fontane, Rome (1637-41).

Concave and convex forms

Curved porches such as Bernini's splendid colonnade at St Peter's, Rome, pediment tops and cornices bent into arches and segments, and spectacular staircases are all baroque features. In some cases, the results seem to defy perspective. The baroque style suited the decorative features of the interior of buildings, in particular churches, as well as the overall structure. In fact it is sometimes difficult to distinguish between the two.

Exaggerated proportions and wall-to-wall decoration

Giant swags, stretched columns, cascades of plaster fruit and flowers – these can be found in baroque buildings. Some of the most extravagant examples of plasterwork, often coloured in pink, white and gold, can be found in the eighteenth-century churches of Bavaria.

Christopher Wren devoted much of his life to the design of St Paul's Cathedral in London.

Later neo-classical architecture

During the eighteenth century neo-classical architecture began to run out of steam. A few visionary architects created some spectacular designs, but for the most part the ideals of the early neo-classical revivalists were in danger of being exhausted.

must know
Domestic architecture in the 1700s
The great majority of medium-sized houses built in Britain and North America were inspired by classical architecture without copying its expensive elements. Houses were often symmetrical, and some had porches, pediments and other decorative features. Many, however, were distinguished by fine brickwork and elegant proportions.

The eighteenth century

The buildings of the baroque period were perhaps the liveliest and the most exhausting members of the classical family. In time fashion always moves on, and after a surfeit of ornament and vigour there was a natural tendency towards elegance and repose.

In spite of eccentric ideas by some architects, mainstream architecture remained neo-classical right up to the middle of the nineteenth century – and in many countries, for nearly a hundred years more. Distinctive new features were introduced, and these can easily be recognized today.

British neo-Palladianism

In Britain, baroque architecture was closely associated with the Tory party, who had ruled during the reign of the autocratic Stuart family. When the Tories lost control and the Hanoverian royal family was imported from Germany, the governing Whig party looked for a way of building that was distinctly unbaroque. For much of the eighteenth century, they chose a simplified version of Palladio's architecture, which to them represented their country's new constitutional monarchy and the pleasures of modern life.

Lord Burlington's villa of the
1720s at Chiswick, to the west of
London, was directly based on
Palladio's Villa Capra.

American classicism

The leaders of the United States, both before and
after 1776, also preferred a version of Palladio's
architecture. An early example is the Capitol in
Williamsburg, Virginia, which has now been rebuilt
in its original form. American Palladianism is
distinguished by fine brickwork, simple windows,
and a variety of slender towers topped by cupolas.
President Thomas Jefferson was also an architect
and designed himself a Palladian house called
Monticello, near Charlottesville in Virginia, at around
the time of the Declaration of Independence.

must know
Thomas Jefferson's architectural career
Jefferson travelled widely in England and France, and was well acquainted with architectural fashion. In addition to his own house, Monticello, he designed the state capitol in Richmond, Virginia (1785–99), which was inspired by the Roman Maison Carrée at Nîmes. His masterpiece is the University of Virginia at Charlottesville (1817–26).

French monumentality

Towards the end of the eighteenth century French politics fell into turmoil, with the revolution of 1789 succeeded first by the chaos of the Terror and then the creation of a new empire under Napoleon. Some visionary French architects designed buildings – mainly unbuilt – that used neo-classical architecture to express feelings of power and mystery. Claude Nicholas Ledoux designed several large scale projects, such as a salt works at Arc-et-Senans (1775–9) and an ideal new town around it called Chaux (partially built by the beginning of the nineteenth century), using elements from the Roman and Greek families that were so terrifyingly over-scaled and simplified that they seem almost barbaric or childlike. Étienne-Louis Boullée also used this simplified style in his designs for vast (and unrealized) buildings which had symbolic, rather

Thomas Jefferson designed his own house, Monticello, which was inspired by Palladio as well as by traditional English domestic architecture.

than practical, layouts. Napoleon himself commissioned buildings in an inflated version of an explicitly Roman manner, such as the Arc de Triomphe in Paris (by Jean-François-Thérèse Chalgrin and Guillaume-Abel Blouet, 1806–36).

Iberian baroque

On some eighteenth-century buildings in Spain and Portugal, particularly churches, one can identify a distinct version of late baroque architecture characterized by extensive rich decoration that flows around otherwise plain external walls. The details of the decoration often have something of the character of patterns made with wet sand. The style was exported to Spanish and Portuguese colonies in Central and South America, where it sometimes combined with local craftsmanship to create a wild style that blurs the traditional distinction between formal and informal architecture.

must know
Étienne-Louis Boullée

Boullée's buildings reflect the rational values of the Enlightenment as well as the political instability and fervour of revolutionary France. His monument to Newton of c 1784 was designed in the form of a gigantic sphere 150 m (492 ft) high – half the height, incidentally, of the Eiffel Tower built a century later. His other famous design is for a library so huge it seems to stretch into infinity.

Living the classical tradition

You now know the essential elements of the history of classical and neo-classical architecture. Now it is time to think about what classical architecture means today, for its traces are everywhere.

must know
Eccentric classicism
The Slovenian architect Jože Plečnik (1872–1957), who was head of the school of architecture at Ljubljana from 1920, created over several decades a remarkable and original interpretation of the neo-classical style. Among his many important works in the city are the National and University Library, and the Church of St Francis, Šiška.

Making sense of classical architecture

Wherever you look, you will find many features drawn from the traditions of the classical family of architecture. You may not necessarily find the same decorative details in buildings close to hand, but you will almost certainly see structures whose proportions and general form have been inspired either by Greek or Roman architecture, or by the many variations devised by later generations. That is especially true if the building is symmetrical in appearance, because symmetry was highly prized by classical designers.

Buildings are often designed to last for hundreds of years and so it is natural for their designers to want to appeal to a sense of the permanent and the established. A feeling of familiarity has often been important too. The varying treatments that different designers have applied over the centuries have also provided us with a wide range of characteristics or 'personalities' within the traditions: there are buildings that seem rough, and others that seem refined; some are seen as democratic types, because of their association with Athens, while others are seen as aristocratic and elevated. It is rather as if by looking at a person's appearance one can gain a picture of their character within.

At all events, you should bear in mind that there is more to the masterpieces of historical architecture than their style. One of your tasks as you learn how to read a building is to address the questions behind the immediate appearance of a structure. Buildings often conjure up associations because of their abstract qualities. The overall proportions of classical buildings, and the careful relationship of their details to each other, were as important to architects as were their ornamentation, materials or decoration. The idea of this neat hierarchy of shapes and forms was so important that it made little difference that they were to be used for new structures such as churches and hospitals rather than pagan temples.

The great number of possibilities that the classical tradition affords means that it will always play a role in the design of the buildings of the future.

want to know more?

Take it to the next level...
- Nineteenth-century public buildings, 108
- Historicizing architecture, 166
- Human nature and personal style, 171

Other sources...
- There is no substitute for a visit to Rome, Florence or Venice, because nearly all the greatest monuments of the renaissance have survived intact.
- A few days spent in the Veneto around Venice are all it takes to become acquainted first-hand with the architecture of Palladio, which has left its mark all over the western world.
- The British Museum in London and the Pergamon Museum in Berlin have fine collections of classical design, including fragments (and more) of ancient architecture.

Further reading
- Have a look at one of the books specializing on the period:

Norberg-Schultz, Christian, *Baroque Architecture* (Electra, 1993)
Spawforth, Tony, *The Complete Greek Temples* (Thames & Hudson, 2006)
Summerson, John, *Architecture in Britain 1530–1830* (Yale University Press, 1993)
Tavernor, Robert, *Palladio and Palladianism* (Thames & Hudson, 1991)
Wilson Jones, Mark, *Principles of Roman Architecture* (Yale University Press, 2003)

3 The gothic tradition

No single great European empire replaced the Roman one, and as a result no single architectural tradition dominated. Instead, each of the developing cultures across the continent began to build in a way that suited its particular climate, using local building materials, and in keeping with its social organization and religious character. Gothic architecture, as this collection of styles is known, flowered between the thirteenth and fifteenth centuries, leaving us with a spectacular variety of churches, cathedrals and manor houses.

The beauty of variety

Mediaeval architecture was not governed by the discipline of standardized orders and proportions as Roman architecture had been. But as masons and craftsmen travelled from town to town and ideas spread across Europe, clear patterns and families of design emerged nonetheless.

must know
Mediaeval
skyscrapers (1)
Mediaeval cathedrals had extremely high ceilings, including:
• Beauvais cathedral: 48 m (157 ft)
• Amiens cathedral: 43 m (140 ft)
• Reims cathedral: 38 m (125 ft)

Defining the gothic family

There is a tremendous variety of form and colour in European architecture over the thousand years that separate the collapse of the Roman Empire towards the middle of the first millennium AD, and the renaissance in the middle of the second. And yet it is possible to classify the many religious and secular buildings using a number of clear categories.

Some of these categories apply best to religious buildings, while others are best seen in the developing domestic architecture of the period. The European peoples, like Roman citizens, invested more money on their places of worship than on their homes, and consequently most homes remained comparatively humble affairs – at least until the later Middle Ages, when some parts of the continent saw periods of relative peace and prosperity. And so the first group of distinguishing features relate mainly to churches, which have generally survived and are more easily found.

Tall vaulted spaces

A vault is a masonry ceiling, and one of the most distinguishing features of the gothic tradition throughout Europe is the way in which churches rise to a great height on slender walls.

The Greeks only knew how to roof a space by placing a timber or stone beam between walls or columns; and although the Romans built arched vaults from stone, these were colossally heavy constructions which required thick walls punctured by small openings. Early church builders throughout Europe essentially imitated the Roman style, and buildings constructed this way are described as Romanesque – 'in the style of the Romans'.

The breakthrough came when masons discovered in the late twelfth century that building an arch with a pointed top allowed them to use less material in a more effective way – and to build higher. As soon as they did, the discovery spread fast across Europe, and buildings began to rise more impressively than before. The style did not in fact have any name at the time, and most of its details were not actually classified until the nineteenth century.

Buttresses

A buttress is a column of stone placed along the outside of a building. Its purpose is to lead the weight of the stone vault away from the walls, because these would otherwise need to be thicker (and therefore be much more expensive and take longer to build).

must know

Mediaeval skyscrapers (2)

English cathedrals were also tall, but not so tall:

- Westminster Abbey: 31 m (102 ft)
- Salisbury cathedral: 25.5 m (85 ft)
- Lincoln cathedral: 25 m (82 ft)

Tall vaults and slender walls, supported by buttresses, are the defining elements of gothic architecture.

must know

When the spire (now long gone) of Lincoln cathedral was completed in the fourteenth century, it was the tallest structure in Europe.

must know
Victorian
rebuilding
It is important to remember that nearly all English mediaeval churches, and many cathedrals, were substantially restored in the nineteenth century. The exterior of the north transept of Westminster Abbey, for example, is entirely Victorian.

PÉGARD. SC.

A buttress attached to a wall acts as a stiffener, allowing larger windows to be cut.

As walls became thinner and vaults higher, builders found that in fact it was more efficient to place a buttress away from the wall. This is because the load of the stone on the roof actually projects its weight at an angle away from the wall, rather than straight down on top of it. These freestanding column-like buttresses were connected to the walls and to each other by a three-dimensional grid of fine stone; when they are like this, they are called flying buttresses.

It is clear both vaults and buttresses will vary from place to place because of the presence of different building materials and skills across Europe. This variety is itself one of the defining characteristics of gothic architecture.

Layout and form

The vaults and buttresses are the most distinguishing features of the gothic family. But there are other aspects which are just as important.

You will have noticed that the great structures of Greek and Roman architecture have often had clear,

The remarkable technology of the flying buttress was one of the most outstanding scientific achievements of the mediaeval era.

symmetrical overall shapes. That is because in classical times, architects believed that the form of a building as a whole was subject to the same abstract rules as, for example, the details of the orders. For them, a building was a kind of symbol of their civilization in its own right: an artificial construction that represented the order and discipline of their civic and military society.

The civilizations of Christian Europe were different. At a time when life was often brutal and dangerous, their peoples highly valued the spiritual aspirations of the church – which in any case exercised considerable political control over them. The result was that their religious buildings, although increasingly sophisticated technically and sometimes arranged in geometrical patterns, were primarily designed to house and to inspire specific acts of worship and church management.

The result in practice was that these buildings were broken up into distinct blocks for different purposes.

The altar

All mediaeval gothic churches are designed around altars, including a central one known as the high altar.

Everything in the main body of a church is therefore planned so that the altars are the centre of attention. In practice this means that the tallest and most impressive space of all will be that around the high altar. In an English cathedral, there is likely to be a vast window behind the altar, and a large open space in front of it to seat the church clergy, who were separated from the congregation in the main body of the church.

Gothic churches were planned around a high altar, although most worshippers could not see it from the nave.

Altars were arranged so that their backs faced the east of the church – which means that in the morning, the eastern windows above them were filled with light.

Projecting chapels

Until the Reformation, when some national churches became independent of the pope and turned towards Protestantism, all churches – even small ones – were filled with altars. Many of these were placed along the walls, and there would be a window or some other kind of architectural feature to mark them.

must know
Stained glass
Mediaeval churches had dark and mysterious interiors. One reason was the stained glass. At Canterbury cathedral there are surviving examples from the fourteenth century showing the murder there of Thomas Becket.

must know
The Reformation
The breakaway of some northern European churches from Roman Catholic control was followed by a purging of anything that might be considered idolatrous from the churches. Antwerp cathedral lost nearly all of over 70 altars in the 1580s.

Leading members of the congregation of a church would sometimes leave money for a special chapel to be built; and the result was that larger gothic churches have one or more projecting rooms around the outside. Sometimes these are clustered in a neat arrangement, for example around the eastern end of the church.

The aisles

Mediaeval churches were designed so that worshippers and pilgrims could make their way through the building towards a particular shrine. This required designing passages called aisles that led around the edges of the major spaces. These routes were often a major part of the design of the building from the outset; many French cathedrals have several parallel aisles which could be used for walking, or subdivided into side chapels with their own altars.

The nave and the clerestories

Stretching westwards in front of the high altar was the nave where the majority of the worshippers stood or sat. Since the nave was often bounded by an aisle on either side, the light had to enter from the north and south at a high level. These windows above the aisles are called clerestories. The nave walls were divided up by arches, and sometimes there was room for a further very narrow high-level aisle, called a triforium.

The gothic plan

It is clear that the arrangement of the different spaces of a church was highly important to the mediaeval builder. There are many words to describe these different areas, although in fact they were not necessarily used at the time the buildings were new.

The apse

The apse is a curved area created when the eastern end of the church projects outwards to create a more distinct and special place around the high altar.

The chancel

The chancel is the area immediately to the west of the high altar; the clergy and the choir sat here, separated from other worshippers by a screen.

The transepts

The transepts, found in cathedrals and the largest churches, are the areas to the north and south of the crossing in front of the chancel. They allowed more worshippers to be present for church services without making the nave impossibly long. The fact that they could not see anything from here was irrelevant – nor could the people in the nave, because of the screen!

Large mediaeval churches were gloomy inside, but high-level windows, called clerestories, admitted some light into the nave.

Transepts also provided possibilities for siting side chapels.

The chapter house

The chapter house was the meeting room for the clergy in a cathedral or abbey, and it was usually located alongside the church itself.

The cloister

The cloister was a covered area for the clergy to walk around in, secluded from the public and protected from the weather.

Porches

Many churches also have porches, not only to shelter from the rain but as a place for statues of saints to welcome worshippers.

Bell towers

Bell towers were for the bells that called the congregation to the services.

There are certain variations in the shapes of these basic structures throughout Europe. French cathedrals, for example, usually have a curved projecting apse at the east end of the church – sometimes surrounded by a complicated structure that incorporates a string of chapels built between the flying buttresses. Amiens cathedral provides a good example of this, but there are other famous ones at Chartres and Reims.

Some people see gothic architecture as being a 'narrative' style – that is, the building appears to be explaining to visitors how it works and what is going on inside. You can guess where the important parts of a church are, because the architecture varies to suit the activity within. Likewise, the decoration of a part of a building will vary in richness depending on how important that part of the structure is to the process of worship. That is another very distinct characteristic of gothic architecture, for in classical architecture builders preferred to maintain a much more even spread of decoration across any one particular wall or feature.

Canterbury cathedral is the principal church of the Anglican communion. Built over centuries, it housed the shrines of three saints.

must know
Gothic ornamental stonework
The different decorative features of the stonework found around gothic walls have curious names, including dog-tooth (a row of X-shaped mouldings), nail head (a row of tiny pyramids), and beak head and cat's head (self explanatory!).

Form and style

Unlike the classical family, where the use of the decorative orders was a major characteristic, it seems that the overall shape and layout of a gothic building are what make it distinct. But gothic architecture of all periods has distinct decorative elements.

must know
Decorated construction
One important principle of gothic architecture was that decoration should be cut out of the fabric of the building, rather than applied onto the surface as classical ornament often is. The pinnacles of a gothic spire are often decorated with crockets, or carved foliage.

The first gothic cathedral

Gothic architecture developed as pre- and early mediaeval builders aimed at creating yet higher and more elegant structures. The first known example of the pointed structural vault and arch can be found at what is now the cathedral of St Denis, the last resting place of the kings of France just north of Paris. Abbot Suger, who was in charge of rebuilding the structure, is often given the credit for masterminding the discovery, which he wrote about at the time.

In some buildings, the masons started using the new pointed style as soon as they had the knowledge to do so – with strange results. At Durham cathedral, for example, a delicate pointed vault was built on top of the sturdy Romanesque columns and walls of the nave. It seems that getting the overall form of a building right was always more important than consistency of architectural style for mediaeval church builders.

The development of gothic art

Gothic buildings provided limitless possibilities for decorative sculpture, and gothic churches of all sizes were filled with decoration of many kinds: stained glass, metalwork, wall paintings, ornamental sculpture and furniture. The style of this ornamental

The Sainte Chapelle in Paris, built in the 1240s, has one of the most breathtaking interiors in mediaeval architecture.

work developed over time, so it is possible to identify the approximate date of a gothic church from its details and ornament.

As a general rule, gothic buildings became lighter and airier as time went by, and sculptural carving on the structure of a building became more sophisticated. A building of the 1150s will be gloomier than one of the 1450s, and the carving more geometrical and less refined.

must know
Ulm Minster
The top of the spire of Ulm's mediaeval cathedral is 161 m (529 ft) above the ground. It was not completed, however, until 1890. Open stonework spires like Ulm's are a feature of the major churches of south-western Germany and Alsace.

The stylistic unity of Salisbury
cathedral is unusual. It was begun
in the early thirteenth century.

The style of the windows of a gothic church are a
good guide to its age.

Tall, pointed narrow windows with little carving

These indicate the first stage of gothic architecture,
from the late twelfth century up to around the end of
the thirteenth century. In England this style is
sometimes called 'early English'.

Broader windows divided into distinct compartments

This second stage of gothic ran for about 50 years
from the end of the thirteenth century and is
sometimes called the 'decorated' phase. The top
compartments of the windows are usually divided up
into smaller openings by ornamental carving.

This splendid church in Ulm, Germany, was started in the fourteenth century but not completed until the nineteenth.

Very broad windows with slender stonework between compartments

This final stage, which was particularly well developed in England, is usually called the 'perpendicular' style. The famous chapel of King's College, Cambridge, designed in the fifteenth and early sixteenth centuries, is often considered the masterpiece of its era.

The narrow lancet windows of Salisbury cathedral indicate the first, 'early English', stage of gothic.

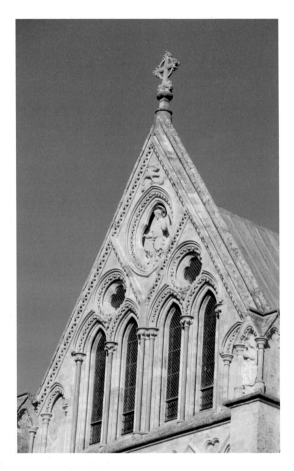

Remember, though, that a gothic church of any size, and especially a large one, will have been built over the course of several decades or even centuries; so a particular window may not necessarily be a guide to the age of the rest of the building.

As with all other elements of decorative gothic work, it is possible to look more carefully and see ever finer distinctions within the main phases of design. But it is more useful at this stage to bear in mind these general categories, and to remember that on the continent of Europe there were many more variations. For example, the most complex style in French gothic architecture, which occurred at about the same time as the English 'perpendicular' style was becoming prevalent, was called the 'flamboyant' style and was characterized by abundant, flame-like patterns in the stonework. Some of these continental styles can best be defined not so much by the windows as by the vaults.

The broad ornamental windows at Exeter cathedral are examples of the second phase of gothic architecture, known as 'decorated'.

Gothic vaults

We have seen that stone vaults are the most important of all the characteristics of the gothic family. It is not surprising, then, that the different styles of these vaults varied over time and place, and they too can be grouped into categories.

Groin vaults

A groin vault is the name of the shape of the structure that results when two semi-circular vaulted ceilings meet each other at right angles. The effect is of a simple pointed crease in the stonework.

Rib vaults

Imagine a ceiling extending inwards to the nave from either side of a broad pointed window. These curved sections of ceiling will meet above the head of the window, and along the centre of the nave they will run up against the sections coming in from the opposite side. All these junctions are neatly trimmed by self-supporting pieces of stone which themselves form pointed arches. This is a rib vault.

At the thirteenth-century cathedral at Salisbury in England you can see a clear example of a typical rib vault from the first or 'early English' period of gothic.

Lierne vaults

Once masons had discovered the principles of pointed vaulting, they started to allow their imagination to inspire them to create highly decorative ceilings. They began to design frameworks of stone arches high up in the air.

At Westminster Abbey, the ceiling that was designed in the mid-thirteenth century is 31 m (102 ft) above the ground, a record for an English mediaeval church.

A rib vault that has extra ribs between the primary ones to form a network of stone like this is called a lierne vault – indeed, the pattern of ribs on a ceiling is called a 'net'.

Fan vaulting

The last of the three stages of gothic, the 'perpendicular', was one that posed special challenges to the masons. The areas to be roofed were wider than earlier, and the walls more slender and more full of windows than ever before.

The roofs designed for these situations were in certain buildings nothing short of spectacular. A thin shell of stonework, supported by integral or separate ribs, was built high up between the walls in the form of a geometrical pattern of concentric circles which descended down into the space to form bosses – 'plugs' – in the stonework that kept the rest of the ceiling in place.

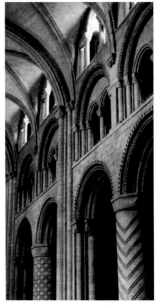

At Durham cathedral a light gothic vault was built over the sturdy Romanesque walls of the nave.

must know
Collar and tie
- A timber that connects two rafters just below the ridge is called a collar.
- A further connecting piece well below the collar is usually called a tie.
- The lowest connecting piece is called a tie-beam, and the post that runs upwards from the tie-beam to the ridge is called a king post.

The chapel of King's College, Cambridge, was founded by King Henry VI and is the best known example of 'perpendicular' gothic.

Roofs like this can be seen both at King's College chapel, and also in the late gothic chapel designed for King Henry VII at the eastern end of Westminster Abbey at the beginning of the sixteenth century.

Folded vaults

Around mediaeval Bohemia (and in particular in today's Czech Republic) there are examples of vaults that have a remarkably modern appearance. They resemble paper folded into complex geometrical shapes, usually without any decoration at all.

Vaulting in Germany

Some masons working in the various German states during the later Middle Ages produced vaults of astonishing sophistication. In the mid-fifteenth-century church of St Lorenz in Nuremburg, for example, there is a delicate roof over the apse of the church that resembles the skeleton of a leaf. In a church at Wesel on the Rhein the stonework appears to peel away from the ceiling to form a delicate suspended pattern of its own.

Some late gothic churches in Germany have particularly beautiful vaults. This is St Anne in Annaberg.

Some of the finest examples can be found in Saxony. At Annaberg, there is another leaf-like ceiling in the church of St Anne: the stems of the 'leaves' twist their way elegantly down towards the piers of the nave. The expertise with stone clearly found its way into secular buildings, too: at Albrechtsburg castle at Meissen, not far from Annaberg, there is a spiral staircase built with similarly sinuous branch-like forms carved from stone.

These examples of complex vault work remind us that the architecture of the Middle Ages was unquestionably the era's greatest technical achievement: one has only to think of the brutal conditions of daily life at the time that these masterpieces were being built.

On the other hand, the mediaeval masons did not always get it right. The first attempt to build a 48 m (157 ft) vault – more than half as high again than that at Westminster Abbey! – at Beauvais north of Paris ended in a disastrous collapse in 1284. Attempts to complete the cathedral were eventually abandoned.

Gothic homes

The larger houses of the mediaeval era were as distinctive as the churches, but at first sight the word 'gothic' does not appear to suit them. Windows with pointed tops are few and far between. However they share a defining characteristic: each important area has its own architectural expression.

How to read a mediaeval house

Like gothic churches, mediaeval houses were built according to a consistent format over a long period in history – which makes identification of their constituent parts quite simple.

Nearly everyone in the Middle Ages lived in such humble accommodation that there is no evidence of it left at all: the only possible solution for most people was to live in a single room constructed of the cheapest and most local building materials (which might be leftover timbers and mud). In England, this was the case right up until the comparative security and prosperity that set in after the defeat of the Spanish Armada, in the middle of the reign of Queen Elizabeth I.

This means that most of our oldest surviving small houses, such as the half-timbered cottages from the fourteenth and fifteenth centuries, were actually the homes of the comparatively well-off, and not anything like as modest as they now seem to us.

Timber houses

Even the surviving timber houses we see today have probably changed a great deal since they were built – the earliest ones would not, for example, have had masonry fireplaces or permanent staircases when they were originally built. These houses, like the stone-built ones common in some areas, then consisted of one single room. Over time increasingly sophisticated methods of framing were invented; the frames were filled with better water and windproof materials; and new features were added for comfort.

Cruck houses

The earliest surviving houses were formed by fixing together pairs of large curved timbers in the form of an inverted V. Each pair was tied together with timber beams at the top and the middle, and then placed over a secure base. These truss-like pairs of

This cruck house in Gloucestershire is mediaeval. Tall tree trunks were tied together to form a frame for the house.

must know
Flemish merchant
architecture
The cities of Flanders, in today's Belgium, have many magnificent buildings in both brick and stone. A perspectival map of 1562 shows the splendid group of public buildings, including the town hall, which dominated the centre of Bruges. Both Leuven and Brussels also have imposing fifteenth-century town halls.

timbers were then connected to each other with more horizontal struts, and the panels filled in with wattle and daub – sticks and mud.

Houses like this, some as old as the thirteenth century, have survived in the area around Herefordshire in the west of England.

The truss

The next stage in the development of the timber house was the truss type. This was a modification of the cruck, for the basic structural system of the house was in effect a series of trusses arranged vertically, with the house formed within the space inside.

The difference between a cruck and a truss house is that the latter no longer depended on the use of a few substantial, tree-sized timbers: it could be made up from posts and beams, with rafters and purlins forming a roof. The result is a more refined looking house.

Box-frame construction

The house could be refined further still if the whole of the wall, rather than merely some of the posts and beams in it, could operate as part of the structure. In building more substantial framed walls with rows of regular timber studs it was possible both to create larger and irregular openings, and to avoid the need for larger timbers to hold the structure together.

You can find many houses of this type all over England and northern Europe where timber was plentiful. They vary from place to place, mainly in the way in which the timber frames were made waterproof. In west Kent, the timber frame was often covered by weatherboarding or tile hanging. As householders became more prosperous, they filled

must know

Decorating a mediaeval manor house

Some mediaeval manor houses have decorated stone vaults in their basements, as well as ornamental gothic stonework around the windows of their chapels or principal rooms. Generally, though, you will not find the type of pointed stonework you associate with a church on a manor house.

the panels with brickwork, sometimes in attractive patterns such as herringbone. Sometimes the whole of the front of a house was lined much later with a neat brickwork wall – so some houses that seem to be Georgian can be much older inside.

The half-timbered construction of these East Anglian houses allowed craftsmen great flexibility in placing windows and doors.

must know
Mediaeval bays
The grander mediaeval manor houses had broad bay windows at one end of their halls in order to provide more light for the high table inside. You can see this feature in the dining halls of many colleges at Oxford and Cambridge.

Features to identify in timber houses include jettying, which is the name for the slight projection of an upper floor over the street. This feature can be quite complicated to construct, and was expensive and wasteful to do, so there is no real explanation for it. By looking carefully at the overall form of a half-timbered house, one can usually work out which was the original part, and where stairs and wings have been added.

The mediaeval manor house

Those prosperous enough to live in a large stone house also built homes which were designed so that they could be easily added to over time. Although the mediaeval manor house seems a great deal more complex than the simple cottage, it is not in fact much more complicated than a series of rooms joined together in a predictable way.

Haddon Hall in Derbyshire began as a simple hall house in around 1370, but has grown in all directions since.

The hall house

From the later Norman period onwards – the twelfth century – those who could afford it began to build houses of stone. They generally built a single large room called a 'great hall' where they could live together with their animals around a central fireplace. In time they added rooms at either end of the hall in order to separate sleeping areas from cooking ones, servants from the landowner's family – and animals from people.

Generally they added a kitchen at one end of the hall, and living accommodation at the other. The result was a house with a plan like an H. When you look at any of these houses, you can readily identify the principal spaces.

The great hall

The great hall formed the central bar of the H. By the thirteenth century, its shape and layout had been largely standardized. The hall was the tallest room of the house, with windows that rose all the way up to a timber roof. A fireplace was by then a built-in feature. The hall often had two doors to the outside and these faced each other down one end of the long sides. Between the doors was a timber screen which

> **must know**
> **Mediaeval furnishings**
> The furniture of even a prosperous mediaeval home was simple but substantial. There was usually little more than a bench, a table, a bed and a storage chest in most rooms.

Great Chalfield Manor is a classic late fifteenth-century hall house that has since become a comfortable home.

kept the wind out of the hall. In some houses this screen has survived.

The kitchen and the buttery

The kitchen eventually moved out of the hall and into a separate chamber at the end of it – usually a room with thick walls and small windows. Adjacent to it was sometimes a buttery – where not butter but *bouteilles* (bottles, in French) were kept.

The parlour

The parlour was the main withdrawing room for members of the house owner's family. In larger houses it eventually became a private dining room.

The solar

The solar was a private room, usually located above the parlour. It was called the solar because it was, by the standards of the Middle Ages, near the *sol* – the sun!

Even when looking at the larger mediaeval houses – such as Haddon Hall in Derbyshire – one can see this arrangement at the centre of the plan. Other rooms were simply added over time to the ends of the wings. The result is a house that spreads along the sides of two courtyards, one either side of the hall.

The splendid palace at Hampton Court, the home of Henry VIII, shows the late mediaeval house at its most expansive.

must know
The mediaeval courtyard
The college courtyards of Oxford and Cambridge with their gothic chapels, halls, and gatehouses – although all greatly restored over the centuries – can give you an excellent idea of what it was like to live in mediaeval surroundings.

Living the gothic tradition

The gothic family, like the classical one, is more than a list of buildings. It too has abstract meanings which have meant much to designers at all times and in all places.

must know

1970s gothic

Plans for several large gothic cathedrals were so ambitious that they were never fully carried out, but one of the most impressive of all was completed in recent times. This was the Anglican cathedral in Liverpool, originally designed by a 22-year-old architect called Giles Gilbert Scott in 1903. The architect died in 1960, but work continued in the original style until 1978. It is the largest Anglican cathedral in Europe.

Making sense of gothic architecture

Gothic buildings were built in quite different conditions from both classical and neo-classical ones. Although many look imposing today, it is an important part of their character that they were built and developed stylistically over a long period of time. In fact it is worth remembering that many of the most splendid gothic buildings were actually much added to, restored, or indeed entirely rebuilt during the nineteenth century. Most of Cologne cathedral in Germany, for example, was built from 1842–80 after its original design drawings were discovered.

By comparing the very different appearance of the classical and gothic families we can see that architecture is not a matter only of style. The members of the two families not only look different: in a sense, they 'behave' differently too: the classical idea of the balanced, symmetrical approach to building is opposed to the organic, narrative gothic one. We shall see why this distinction matters in the following chapters, because to some extent a battle of methods and approaches to historic buildings comes to characterize the architecture of the nineteenth century.

Before we leave the gothic tradition, however, it is worth reflecting again on the more general lessons that we can learn from its architecture. As with the architects of Rome and Greece, we know very little – in fact, even less – about the intentions of those who built them. We do, however, know that the technical and artistic quality of the best mediaeval buildings was by far and away the most sophisticated technological and scientific achievement of the peoples that built them. That means not only that buildings were important to them: they were quite possibly more important than anything else. And that is part of the lasting appeal of gothic design: it strove to incorporate so much in its buildings that was worth living for.

want to know more?

Take it to the next level...
- Human nature and personal style, 171
- The gothic revival, 126
- Organic architecture, 140

Other sources...
- A visit to any of the great English manor houses that are open to the public is enough to establish a clear idea of how the hall house was designed and developed. The National Trust for England and Wales owns several wonderful examples, including Cotehele House in Cornwall, Great Chalfield Manor in Wiltshire, and Melford Hall in Suffolk.
- Likewise, when you next visit a great gothic church of any period – including a nineteenth-century one – try to establish what exactly the link is between the parts of the architecture and the religious traditions within. If you have an opportunity to visit a mediaeval church, try to work out when the different periods of building began according to the decorative details of the stonework.
- Look at mediaeval paintings, especially of the fifteenth and sixteenth centuries, to get an idea of how halls, kitchens and bedchambers were occupied at the time. Some Flemish painters captured these interiors in great detail.

Further reading
- Have a look at one of the books specializing on the period:

Brown, R.J., *The English Country Cottage* (Robert Hale, 1979)
Brunskill, R.W., *Vernacular Architecture: an Illustrated Handbook* (Faber & Faber, 2000)
Coldstream, Nichola, *Medieval Architecture* (Oxford University Press, 2002)
Cooper, N., *Houses of the Gentry 1480–1680* (Yale University Press, 1999)

4 The nineteenth century

In some ways, nineteenth-century architecture has had more influence on the way buildings look now than that of the last hundred years. That is because architects were then faced with an explosion of new building types and materials which forced them to experiment with new ideas. Buildings from this period may seem to resemble the historical architecture from the classical and gothic families, but very often the resemblance is only skin deep.

New buildings for new uses

Wherever you live, you can find evidence of the nineteenth-century building boom. In any historical town there will be buildings that testify to the value placed on architecture by Victorians, who believed in its importance as a means of promoting civic and commercial values.

What is special about the nineteenth century?

During the nineteenth century there was a great deal of discussion by architects and others about using and reinventing stylistic ideas from the classical and gothic families of design. Sometimes, and particularly in Britain, the decision to use one of these traditional styles was passionately challenged. But the most characteristic achievement of nineteenth-century architecture throughout the world is the dramatic adaptation of historical architecture to suit new building types. Most kinds of public institution, including parliament buildings, town halls, large schools, hospitals, prisons and railway stations, were designed for the first time.

An important part of reading a building from the nineteenth century is finding out exactly what it was built for – because its precise purpose tells us so much about Victorian life and society, and why architecture was so important to them.

Creating a modern society

The Palace of Westminster in London is a well known building that exemplifies the way in which architects were creating new and complex types of structure in the mid-nineteenth century. It was built to replace a chaotic jumble of old buildings after a major fire in 1834, and the long process of designing and furnishing its replacement required thinking through the activities and methods of parliamentary procedure to the last detail. The result was in its day the most sophisticated and indeed complicated building ever built.

Looking at nineteenth-century buildings all around will give you a valuable insight into changes in daily life immediately before and during the Victorian period. It will also remind you of the close link between architecture and politics. As elected local authorities began to establish their control of cities, they spent money on new town halls both as places of debate and administration but also as symbols of their new power. Other nineteenth-century building types to look out for include:

The Palace of Westminster was designed by Charles Barry, assisted by Augustus Pugin. It has come to symbolize British democracy.

must know

Museums

It is only recently that we have begun to rival the museum-building mania of the nineteenth century. London alone saw the construction of splendid and vast new buildings for the British Museum, the National Gallery and National Portrait Gallery, the Natural History Museum and the Victoria and Albert Museum.

Museums

An act of parliament in the early years of Queen Victoria's reign allowed local authorities to raise money from householders to build museums as a way of demonstrating the values of culture and history. Many other countries soon recognized the importance of national museums.

Prisons and workhouses

Prisons had traditionally been housed in an accumulation of old buildings and run for profit by private managers. There was a great deal of debate in early nineteenth-century Britain and America as to how to run them on more healthy, efficient and productive lines – not least because there was by this period a serious shortage of prison space. Workhouses had previously been small, local institutions which temporarily housed those who could not work; after 1834 they were transformed

The British Museum in London, designed by Robert Smirke in the Ionic order, took more than 20 years to build.

into a national network of prison-like structures, and their main purpose was essentially to frighten people back to work. Many of these workhouses still exist – transformed into hospitals or even luxury housing!

Churches and cathedrals

There are several reasons why the nineteenth century saw an explosion in church building in England. The first was that most churches were mediaeval and were in a bad physical state – and the religious revival of the first half of the century aimed to rebuild them as splendid and awe-inspiring places of worship. As church attendance grew, so did the need for new churches and eventually for new cathedrals. The second reason was that church leaders realized that an impressive church building is an important assertion of authority in any town. And thirdly, and very significantly, members of religious groups other than the established church were finally given civil rights equal to those of the majority, and began to raise money to build new buildings.

Hospitals

All the new industrial societies suffered badly from disease, such as the cholera outbreak which killed

must know
New schools
Victorian legislation often directly resulted in major new architecture programmes. William Gladstone's Education Act of 1870, for example, established locally controlled boards that at once set about building new schools across the country.

some 18,000 people in London in 1848–50. It was only towards the middle of the nineteenth century that scientists began to identify the way in which diseases were transmitted, and great efforts were made to experiment with the isolation of patients in healthily designed wards. The resulting buildings were not always successful medically, but they were often large and impressive.

Railway structures

Perhaps the most significant of all the new building types of the period were the railway structures. George Stephenson's 'Locomotion No 1' ran from Stockton to Darlington in the north-east of England from 1825, and in a very short period of time railways were built all over the country – and all over the world.

The first railway terminus is often thought to be Crown Street Station in Liverpool, which was connected by Stephenson's famous 'Rocket' to Manchester. The station is long gone, but there are many structures all over the country dating from the first decades of the new transportation system. These include not only stations but railway hotels, bridges, aqueducts, cuttings, tunnels, and various service buildings such as trainsheds and depot structures. Some buildings have even been converted into residences.

Why the railway is so important

The railway is particularly important to the history of architecture because it revolutionized so many different aspects of daily life. It had never before been possible, for example, to commute speedily and conveniently between home and the workplace: the result was that very soon, many people were able to live outside the centre of cities and could afford to buy themselves larger homes on the cheaper land more readily available there. In this way, the suburb was born. Furthermore, railway structures soon became very large indeed, and whole landscapes were transformed. Most people had never seen anything so powerful in their life as a railway engine, nor any building as impressive as a modern railway station.

But the railways are important in another way too: they affected the life and work of the Victorian professional. It was possible for an architect to travel long distances speedily and safely, working along the way, which meant that it was possible to build up a professional practice that was much larger than ever before. One of the most influential and famous British architects of the period, Sir George Gilbert Scott, is often thought to be the founder of the modern architectural practice, with a large staff working on buildings all over the country. It is therefore appropriate that he designed one of the most popular station structures of all time: the hotel and railway offices block at the front of St Pancras Station in London, now the terminus of the Eurostar route to Paris.

St Pancras Station, fronted by Scott's Midland Grand Hotel, is one of the most impressive railway structures in the world.

must know

The Stephensons

George Stephenson was born near Newcastle in 1781, and adapted steam technology to the idea of a carriage drawn on tracks to create the first practical locomotive. His son Robert was born in 1803, and designed bridges across the world, including the Victoria Bridge over the St Lawrence River at Montréal.

The Victorian professional

We have seen that new types of buildings were created as a result of political change and scientific progress. But the people behind the new buildings were changing too, and the new way in which architects saw themselves soon began to affect their designs.

**must know
Victorian
architectural
competitions**
Victorian competitions
were sometimes
disasters, often
followed by allegations
that a jury had chosen
its favourite architect
regardless of the merits
of his scheme. The
competitions for the
Foreign Office and the
Law Courts in London
were particularly
catastrophic. The stress
of building the Law
Courts eventually
hastened their
architect's death.

Building a modern society

Large buildings are expensive to build, but they were necessary to provide decent working conditions for the substantial groups of people who now had to work together under one roof. No government likes to spend money, but sometimes they simply had to in order for their reforms to work. As the state began to intervene in more and more sectors of life – including for example culture, science and education, which had previously been private concerns – countries across Europe and the Americas began to spend enormous sums providing buildings to house state employees.

Some very fine (and very costly) buildings emerged from this process: some of them have even become almost symbolic of the country where they were built. We have already mentioned the Palace of Westminster. Here are some others:

The Louvre, Paris
The Louvre had traditionally been a royal palace, but it was greatly expanded to form government offices in the 1860s and 70s. The resulting complex was seen at the time as a model of a modern government office block.

The Capitol, Washington

The great dome and twin debating chambers of the Capitol are part of an enormous administrative structure that took decades to complete. It was begun in 1792, but was partially rebuilt and greatly enlarged over time, mainly to designs by British-born architect Benjamin Latrobe. It was not completed until 1867.

The national parliament buildings of the nineteenth century rivalled each other in splendour and scale. This is the Capitol in Washington.

The Foreign and Commonwealth Office, London

Today's Foreign and Commonwealth Office in Whitehall, alongside Downing Street, was actually originally built in 1860–75 as a complex of different government departments. Its neo-classical style was controversial among architects at the time.

The Palace of Justice, Brussels

This huge building was built in 1866–83 to house a function which was greatly expanded throughout the western world during the nineteenth century – a modern and largely transparent national system of justice. The result is an enormous and sophisticated complex which is intended to impress on visitors the power of the state.

The Stock Exchange, Amsterdam

A very unusual and imaginative late nineteenth-century building by the great Dutch architect H.P. Berlage, this impressive structure became a symbol of the commercial importance of an historic trading nation.

Architects, builders, surveyors and engineers

We have seen that nineteenth-century politics resulted in new occupations, and these in turn required new buildings. But the way in which designers of buildings were organized as a profession changed too, with far reaching results for architecture.

Until the early nineteenth century, architecture was not distinctly defined as a profession. Some people who designed buildings were amateurs, who would not have seen themselves as working people: they drew their ideas from illustrated books about classical architecture, and adapted the designs they saw there into new houses or public buildings – often for members of their own social circle. Others might well have been what we would today call building contractors, essentially employed to arrange the building of a structure and providing a design for it as part of the service they offered. Another group of people would nowadays be considered more like engineers: they developed a skill for designing complicated structures such as bridges, and were happy to add decoration to them in order to make them look more refined.

This changed over the course of the early nineteenth century. Architects, civil engineers and eventually surveyors of various kinds formed themselves into distinct professions, setting themselves codes of conduct and distancing themselves from the business side of building. Architects did this to make it clear that they had no personal financial interest from a building project, and thus, like a doctor or a lawyer, were there in order primarily to serve their client. Furthermore, they were faced with a much more complicated building process, and they saw it as part of their duty to become familiar with the new technology involved in building. Being a member of a professional institute made it clear that an architect was committed to high modern standards of design, rather than the expediencies common in much of the building world.

must know

The water closet
The first water closet was designed by Sir John Harrington during the reign of Queen Elizabeth I, but the invention did not catch on until Joseph Bramah patented his own version in 1778. The S-bend, the trap and the flush were invented at the beginning of the nineteenth century.

Recent inventions that Victorians would expect to find in their new home would include:

Water closets

Most new houses, and certainly the homes of a professional, a businessman or a skilled tradesman, would most likely have had at least one and possibly two water closets by the 1840s. The discovery of the S-bend, which prevented smells from rising up into the room by a layer of water, greatly improved the situation.

A modern kitchen

An eccentric character called Count Rumford, who fought on the losing side in the American War of

From the 1840s the Victorian kitchen was increasingly well equipped with modern technology.

Independence and subsequently made his living as an inventor in Europe, is sometimes credited with the design of the first fitted kitchens: he designed all-in-one stove units that could be inserted into the old fireplace of a kitchen. The backstairs areas of even medium-sized houses grew enormously as Victorian house owners required special spaces for each of various domestic activities, from shoe cleaning to cider storage.

Central heating

One of the reasons for the attention paid to methods of central heating in the larger Victorian houses was the contemporary interest in exotic plants – which needed to be kept in conservatories at high temperatures. Large new churches needed heating, too. Central heating was not unusual by the 1860s, and early systems circulated hot steam through very wide cast iron pipes.

Damp proofing

Architects had traditionally used impermeable materials such as slate to prevent damp rising up through a building from the earth, but by the mid-1850s more sophisticated systems, such as waterproof renders and ventilated cavities, were being introduced.

Gas and electrical lighting

A modern house of the 1840s would be designed for gas lighting, and electricity had superseded it by the end of the nineteenth century.

A building disaster

No one would think today that Buckingham Palace, the London residence of the Queen, could ever have been described as a controversial building. Most of it, including the wing lived in by the Queen's family and the rooms that face the garden, were designed for King George IV by John Nash, the architect renowned for the elegant neo-classical buildings around Regent's Park, and the new streets such as Regent Street that led up to them.

In fact at the time, the 1820s, the building was considered a catastrophe: it was badly built, it provided insufficient accommodation for state

must know
King George IV
King George IV, who reigned from 1820-30, was possibly the British king with the greatest interest in architecture. As well as commissioning Buckingham Palace from John Nash, he developed the royal estates in London on a grand scale, and also built avidly at Windsor and in Brighton.

occasions, it looked slightly odd to critical eyes, and – most seriously – it went wildly over budget. As a result of the parliamentary enquiry that followed, architects began to realize that in future they could be held personally responsible for technical failures and for wasting their clients' money. This had a profound impact on the way architects saw their own professional duties.

The building of Buckingham Palace was originally something of a disaster, and spelled the end of architect John Nash's career.

New materials

Architects have always enjoyed experimenting with the spaces inside a building as much as with the design of the exterior walls. Technological developments put many new possibilities within their reach, as well as allowing their clients to commission ever bigger buildings.

must know
Wrought iron and cast iron
Wrought iron technology, whereby the hot metal was forged into shape by the blacksmith, had existed since time immemorial, but cast iron was a seventeenth-century invention that with the Industrial Revolution became a major component in buildings. Unlike wrought iron, it was strong in compression – but it was correspondingly weak in tension. Many buildings therefore used both.

Cast iron and glass architecture

Just as there were new building types, there were also new building materials. The two go hand in hand, because some new types of structure such as railway termini required large roofs covering unobstructed spaces. These could not be built using solid masonry, so architects were obliged to consider using the type of solutions that engineers were developing for industrial buildings, most notably frames built up from cast iron standardized units. These might have decorative elements in timber or wrought iron, and were easily glazed with newly available large sheets of plate glass.

A breakthrough came with Joseph Paxton's design for the Crystal Palace in Hyde Park, London. This was constructed to house the 1851 Great Exhibition, a display of British and foreign manufactured goods which attracted millions of visitors from all over the world. People found the colourful, dazzling interior of this 563 m (1848 ft)-long building to be an exciting experience – perhaps rather like arriving for the first time today in one of the largest and most modern airport terminals. And yet astonishingly the Crystal Palace was constructed on site in just over three months.

The Crystal Palace was dismantled, relocated, and eventually burned down in 1936, but there are many surviving buildings which illustrate the dramatic effects that architects could achieve using adventurous structural systems:

Paddington Station, London

The splendid train shed at Paddington Station was designed by the great engineer Isambard Kingdom Brunel and built soon after the Crystal Palace. It was one of a series of dramatic new railway stations of the 1850s and 1860s.

The popular success of the Crystal Palace in 1851 transformed attitudes towards building in cast iron and glass.

must know
The Crystal Palace
The Crystal Palace was originally built in Hyde Park close to where the Albert Memorial now stands. Six million people visited it, and with the resulting profit the government bought and developed the area around South Kensington. The palace itself was rebuilt on a larger scale in Sydenham, South London.

must know
Railway stations in New York

New York once had two railway termini to rival London's. Grand Central Station has survived and was recently restored, but the majestic Pennsylvania Railroad Station by McKim Mead and White (1902–11), which covered more than 3 hectares (8 acres), was needlessly demolished in the mid-1960s.

The Palm House, Kew Gardens, Surrey

The neo-classical architect Decimus Burton worked with Irish iron founder and engineer Richard Turner to design this magnificent conservatory in 1844.

Galleria Vittorio Emanuele II, Milan, Italy

Designed by Giuseppe Mengoni, this structure of 1865–7 took the form of an internal street enclosed by a glazed roof. It must surely be the ancestor of many modern shopping centres.

This covered shopping street in Milan, the Galleria Vittorio Emanuele II, exemplifies the civic pride of many nineteenth-century cities.

Bibliothèque Ste.-Geneviève, Paris

This library in central Paris was completed in 1850 and exploited the potential of cast iron to create airy, elegant spaces, with results more reminiscent of a church than of a civil institution. The architect was Henri Labrouste.

The Bibliothèque Ste.-Geneviève in Paris, designed by Henri Labrouste, demonstrated how an elegant interior could be created from industrial components.

must know
Parisian shops
Several splendid new stores in Paris, particularly the Grands Magasins du Printemps (1881–5) and Samaritaine (1905–6), used iron technology to create spectacular open spaces where crowds of shoppers could compare goods in comfort.

The Ritz Hotel, London

The Ritz Hotel on Piccadilly looks like a masonry building in the French neo-classical style, but in fact the stone cladding masks the first steel-framed building in London. The architects were Mewès and Davis, 1903–6. Steel was used in buildings for various purposes from the 1880s onwards.

The growth of the engineer

Architects could not usually themselves keep up with technical developments, and as the processes of calculation and design of iron and steel structures became more complicated they increasingly relied on engineers for help in realizing their ideas. The result was the growth of the profession of the civil engineer, without which many of the most visionary projects of the last 150 years would have been impossible.

Isambard Kingdom Brunel and Robert Stephenson, the son of the locomotive pioneer, were both mechanical engineers who turned their hand to architectural structures such as bridges and stations, sometimes with the help of architects. Others were clearly talented designers in their own right.

must know
The Brunels
Marc Brunel was born in France in 1796, and after a period in New York settled in London, where he designed the Thames Tunnel, today a railway tunnel, at Wapping. His son Isambard was born in Portsmouth in 1806 and became engineer to the Great Western Railway in 1833.

The famous 300 m (985 ft)-high Eiffel Tower in Paris was designed as a temporary structure for an exhibition in the city in 1889 by the engineer Gustave Eiffel, but it has remained ever since as much because of its architectural beauty as for its practical use as a massive city-centre antenna.

Engineer Gustave Eiffel designed the Eiffel Tower for an international exhibition of 1889, but its popularity saved it from demolition.

must know
Cast iron shop and office facades
Widely (but wrongly) believed at the time to be safer than timber or masonry for industrial buildings, facades made of cast iron and glass can be seen in many nineteenth-century industrial cities, such as Chicago, Liverpool and Glasgow.

The gothic revival

The great majority of large new buildings in the western world constructed in the nineteenth century were neo-classical – except in Britain. Here a new way of designing was developed which subsequently influenced architects everywhere.

Augustus Pugin

The young architect and designer Augustus Pugin and his followers transformed British architecture. A deeply religious (although eccentric) Roman Catholic, he yearned for the days when gloriously decorated mediaeval churches dominated daily life. This led him to investigate exactly what these

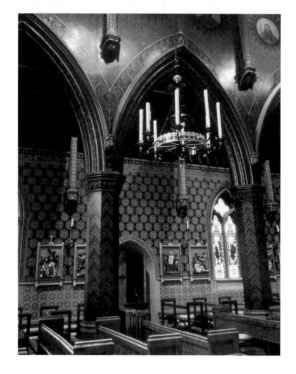

St Giles' Church, Cheadle, is considered one of Pugin's greatest masterpieces. It closely resembled an authentic mediaeval church.

Pugin's own house in Ramsgate, the Grange of 1843-4, demonstrated a completely new way of designing.

buildings had been like in their heyday before the Reformation. His conclusion was that unlike neo-classical structures, gothic buildings had been designed on the principles of structural efficiency, and that the layout of the building on the inside was more important than presenting a tidy symmetrical facade to the street.

Pugin presented his ideas in a series of illustrated books, and the impact they had was tremendous. It was only comparatively recently that architects had begun to appreciate the mediaeval buildings of England, because most of them were in so bad a physical state that it was difficult to work out their original form. In fact it had not been until the early nineteenth century that anyone had been able to

must know
The beginning of functionalism?
Pugin's famous declaration 'that there should be no features about a building which are not necessary for convenience, construction, or propriety' appeared in his book *The True Principles of Pointed or Christian Architecture* in 1841. It is sometimes considered to herald a modern, functional approach to architecture.

work out how mediaeval builders had designed the pointed arch. So Pugin's message was greeted with excitement by those who were bored of the neo-classical style and now felt they were tapping a rich vein in the cultural history of their own country.

Pugin at home

Pugin's churches were the first that actually resembled genuine mediaeval buildings for several hundred years. Some of them are dramatic: the best known is perhaps St Giles', Cheadle, in Staffordshire, with its soaring spire. The decorative work which covered the whole of the Palace of Westminster was also an astonishing achievement. But the most remarkable part of his legacy is the way in which architects began to look at every single detail of the buildings they designed in a new light. They saw it as their duty to turn away from industrialized

Gothic revival architects combined modern materials with mediaeval-style forms. This is the University Museum in Oxford from the 1850s.

components such as cheap ironmongery and imitation stone, and to aspire to the highest standards of craftsmanship.

Pugin's insistence that a house should be designed according to a modern, practical layout, and that all the technical details in it should be logical and consistent, came to be one of the dominant ideas in subsequent architectural history. If your own home was built in the twentieth century, it is quite likely that it has some of Pugin's ideas in it. Look at the arrangement of the windows from the outside, for example: if they are arranged to suit the rooms inside rather than to create a regular facade, you have already identified a Puginian influence. Tall roofs to throw off the rain and the big chimneys that can often be seen in private housing estates of the 1960s and 1970s are also one of his trademarks: he hated the impractical, almost flat, roofs in Georgian houses, and the way their designers tried to hide the chimneys because they did not know how to make them look like parts of Greek temples.

The spread of gothic

Pugin's ideas were rapidly adopted by ambitious young architects, and since they suited the ideas of the promoters of the religious revival across England it was not long until some impressive new buildings were erected in the gothic style. We have already come across the spectacular building at St Pancras Station in London. Others include:

Manchester Town Hall

Designed by Alfred Waterhouse and built from 1867–77, this building unmistakeably demonstrates the growing power of Britain's great industrial cities.

Trinity Church was once the tallest building in Manhattan. It was designed by Richard Upjohn using Pugin's version of gothic.

Keble College, Oxford

This college with its imposing chapel was built from the late 1860s to demonstrate the power of the religious revival in Oxford; it was intended to imitate mediaeval colleges but on a grand scale.

The Law Courts, London

A very expensive group of buildings, designed by the respected church architect George Edmund Street following a competition in 1866, which demonstrated how the gothic style could suit a complex modern building. It went up at the same period as the Palace of Justice in Brussels.

American architect H.H. Richardson developed a very personal interpretation of the Romanesque style. This is a detail from his Sever Hall at Harvard.

Churches everywhere

Amazingly, almost every mediaeval church in England was restored or entirely rebuilt. Many completely new ones went up, including a cathedral at Truro in Cornwall designed by John Loughborough Pearson.

The gothic revival abroad

Although it was in England that the gothic revival had the most impact, there are also some very notable buildings in other countries – particularly in North America. The Episcopal Cathedral of St John the Divine in New York, which was started in 1892 but never entirely completed, is a fine example. There are many other gothic revival buildings across the continent, including:

Trinity Church, New York

Designed in Pugin's style by Richard Upjohn and built from 1840-6, this famous church is one of several that today make a striking contrast with their more modern and massive neighbours in Manhattan.

Sever Hall, Harvard

H.H. Richardson designed many unusual structures, including this college building in Cambridge, Massachussetts, of 1878-80.

Dominion Parliament Buildings, Ottawa

Canada's parliament was originally designed by British-born architect Thomas Fuller and Chilion Jones in the gothic style and constructed from 1861-7, although it was rebuilt after a fire in 1916. The Hungarian parliament building in Budapest is also gothic.

The arts and crafts movement

Although the gothic revival was largely a British movement, its later stage, the arts and crafts movement, influenced designers worldwide. Its architects took a relaxed view of style, choosing details from all branches of the classical and gothic families in order to create a gentle kind of architecture.

must know
Edwin Lutyens
During his lifetime, Edwin Lutyens (1869-1944) was considered Britain's greatest living architect. His early buildings were in an arts and crafts style, but by the early twentieth century he had begun to develop an original version of neo-classicism, characterized by complex proportional systems. He designed the viceroy's, now president's, palace at New Delhi, India.

The architects of the arts and crafts movement

The movement began in earnest in the 1860s as popular taste began to react against the often stern nature of the gothic revival. Most of the arts and crafts architects were young men who greatly admired Pugin, but who felt that his principles could be achieved in other ways. In particular, they looked to traditional English village architecture from the late gothic and early neo-classical periods, and adapted their often picturesque forms for modern buildings.

Identifying the various members of the traditional families in these late nineteenth-century buildings can be fun. One might find a large elegant window

Philip Webb's first building was designed for William Morris. It is also often considered to be the first arts and crafts house.

from the days of Queen Anne imposed on an elevation that otherwise looks Tudor. This type of architecture was inspiring to architects all over the world at the time, as it showed that so long as high standards of craftsmanship were maintained, one could produce buildings that were familiar and comfortable but also quite new in appearance. Houses built at this time were characteristically much brighter and more cheerful within than some earlier Victorian houses had been. In some cases, too, the quality of the workmanship – always an important element with Pugin's supporters – was astonishingly high.

There were many important architects who designed in this way, and their designs were widely published abroad so that their ideas soon spread. They include:

C.F.A. Voysey's houses combined a consistent use of materials and forms with delicate and original detailing. This is Broadleys, overlooking Windermere.

must know
Voysey and films
Voysey's houses have
been popular with
filmmakers: Broadleys
appears in *The French
Lieutenant's Woman*,
and a house called
Norney, near
Shackleford in Surrey,
features in *Carrington*.
Interestingly, his niece
was married to the
famous 1930s film star
Robert Donat.

Charles Rennie Mackintosh's
idiosyncratic style was
appreciated more in Europe than
in his home city of Glasgow.

Philip Webb

Webb designed Red House, to the south-east of
London, for his friend the designer William Morris in
1859. Plainly and honestly built of red brick, and
with a mixture of different historical references, it is
widely recognized as the first arts and crafts house.
Webb always insisted on the highest quality of
workmanship and continued to experiment in his
work until he retired at the end of the century.

Richard Norman Shaw

The designer of a series of large romantic country
houses, Shaw also designed New Scotland Yard,
then the headquarters of the Metropolitan Police,
alongside the Thames near the Palace of
Westminster.

C.F.A. Voysey

The distinctive style of Voysey's architecture
scarcely changed across his working life, which
continued up to the First World War. His houses
were long and low, with white walls, bold
buttresses and continuous strips of windows. He
was thus – to his disgust – often seen as the
harbinger of the modernist architecture of the
twentieth century.

M.H. Baillie Scott

Although his work is less immediately identifiable
from the outside than that of some other arts and
crafts architects, Baillie Scott is significant as the
man who developed the idea of the flexible
interior plan, the precursor of the open plans of
later generations.

Charles Rennie Mackintosh

The Scottish architect Mackintosh was an idiosyncratic designer who became famous internationally, especially in Vienna where he was welcomed enthusiastically by young artists.

want to know more?

Take it to the next level...
- Monumental architecture, 156
- Very late 'Victorians', 140
- John Ruskin, 172

Other sources...
- Go to your local church and look out for the signs of Victorian architecture and design. In a mediaeval building, you may well be able to identify those parts which were restored in the nineteenth century. By comparing Victorian churches, you can learn which aspects of their design were thought important at the time; and in a recent church you can identify the modern descendants of characteristic Victorian fittings.
- If you are near a nineteenth-century railway station, try to see if you can make a list of all the different aspects of design which had to be thought out from scratch when the technology was new: there may be different kinds of office and storage areas, signs, ramps, bridges, and perhaps a café.
- Look at nineteenth-century maps of your nearest town centre in your local history library in order to see how the area developed, and what the impact of large new buildings must have been.

Further reading
- Have a look at one of the books specializing on the period:

Atterbury, Paul & Wainwright, Clive (eds), *Pugin: a Gothic Passion* (Yale University Press, 1994)

Davey, Peter, *Arts and Crafts Architecture* (Phaidon, 1995).

Dixon R. & Muthesius S., *Victorian Architecture* (Thames & Hudson, 1978)

Middleton R. & Watkin D., *Architecture of the Nineteenth Century* (Electa, 2003)

5 Architecture since 1900

After the turmoil of the nineteenth century, architecture began to develop in different and surprising ways. Buildings in new and unfamiliar forms appeared all over the world, often as a response to local situations and following short-lived fashions. With the monopoly of the two great families of design broken, architects felt that they could experiment. And yet in many respects, it is still possible to identify distant family traits in even the most unlikely buildings.

The turn of the century

There was, of course, no sudden change in architecture in 1900. On the other hand, there were a number of developments which contributed to an air of experimentation even before the First World War broke out in 1914.

must know
Skyscrapers
The Wainwright Building of 1890 was ten storeys high, but steel frames and efficient lifts meant that buildings soon could rise much higher. The first truly high-rise skyscraper in New York was the Woolworth Building of 1911–13, which was 241 m (792 ft) high. Within 20 years it was dwarfed by the Chrysler Building (319 m, 1048 ft) and the Empire State Building (381 m, 1250 ft).

Frank Lloyd Wright

The great American architect Frank Lloyd Wright enjoyed one of the longest careers in the history of architecture. Born in 1867, he joined an established Chicago architect firm in his early twenties, started designing independently in 1889, and continued up to 1959 – when he was over 90.

The fact that Wright had already launched his career by 1900 suggests that he was rooted in the nineteenth century. He certainly experienced some of its changes such as rapid urbanization and the incorporation of sophisticated technology into office buildings at first hand. Working for Louis Sullivan in Chicago, he believed he witnessed the moment the skyscraper was born – when Sullivan unveiled his design for the Wainwright Building in St Louis, Missouri, in 1890. At the same time, he was sympathetic of the aims of the English arts and crafts movement. Like them, he placed a high value on good building materials and craftsmanship, and he rejected altogether the formal neo-classical and gothic styles. On the other hand, he welcomed opportunities to experiment with new materials such as reinforced concrete.

In fact he claimed that he designed with 'style' rather than 'a style', and his buildings do not fit easily into either of the two traditional western families. He was a connoisseur of Japanese art, and if anything his architecture reflects some aspects of Japanese design: long low buildings, projecting roofs, and much use of grids both as planning and decorative devices.

Wright's architecture changed in appearance several times over his long life:

Winslow House, Chicago, 1893-4
The first of Wright's famous houses, this bold suburban villa was planned around a series of unusual flowing spaces designed around a large central hearth.

Robie House, Chicago, 1908-10
Wright called houses like these 'Prairie Houses': brick built, almost exaggeratedly long and low, and composed of a series of simple elegant forms stacked up rather like a battleship. This one was perhaps the most Japanese in appearance of all of Wright's designs.

Millard House, Pasadena, California, 1923
For a while Wright experimented with specially designed ornamental concrete blocks, using motifs that look as if they were drawn from the Mayan civilization of Central America.

Fallingwater, Bear Run, Pennsylvania, 1934-7
One of the most famous houses of the twentieth century, Fallingwater is a masterpiece created from concrete levels cantilevered out over a waterfall.

Jacobs House, Madison, Wisconsin, 1936-7
Some of Wright's later houses, which he named 'Usonian' after the U.S.A., were comparatively small

Louis Sullivan's Wainwright Building in St Louis was the world's first skyscraper. It was designed in 1890.

and delicate structures with ingenious plans and
built of simple unornamented materials.

Organic architecture

Wright liked to use the term 'organic architecture', which
for him meant a way of building that was sympathetic to
the natural lines of the landscape and its flora. Although
many architects towards the middle of the twentieth
century came to see themselves as organic designers,
those who first began to experiment with flowing lines
were late 'Victorians' like Wright himself.

In some respects, organic architecture shares some
characteristics of the gothic family. Individual rooms
are often expressed, and windows and roofs fall into
places that seem 'natural' to the architect. Brick and
ornamental carved stone were popular materials. On
the other hand, many organic buildings have irrational,
even wild ornamentation, and some architects liked to
create curious shapes from wrought iron.

Some other very late 'Victorians'

Antoni Gaudí, who died in 1926, spent the last
decades of his life working on the design and
construction of the Sagrada Familia cathedral in

The home designed for Frederick
C. Robie in 1908–10 is a remarkable
example of Frank Lloyd Wright's
'Prairie House' style.

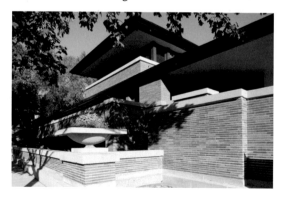

Wright designed Fallingwater for the Kauffmann family in 1934–5. It is one of his most breathtaking and original creations.

Barcelona – which will still not be complete for many years. His many eye-catching constructions in the city perhaps owe something to the 'wet sand' appearance of Iberian baroque, but constructionally they are often extremely sophisticated.

Peder Vilhelm Jensen-Klint designed the Grundtvig Church to the north of central Copenhagen in 1913. Incorporating ideas drawn from traditional Danish architecture, it is perhaps the most striking early twentieth-century building in the country.

Hector Guimard, who was born in the same year as Wright, designed the entrances to the Metro stations with their flowing, botanical shapes in Paris between 1900 and 1904. They have become one of the symbols of Paris.

Michel de Klerk, a young Dutch architect, designed some unusual housing in Amsterdam between 1910 and 1920, using brick to create distinctive and memorable forms.

Antoni Gaudí's architecture was inspired by the gothic tradition but highly personal. His cathedral in Barcelona is still under construction.

Erich Mendelsohn

Very few architects have managed to create an altogether new architectural style – a new family, whose characteristics enter the mainstream. Erich Mendelsohn was one of these. His designs turned purely contemporary phenomena, from Einstein's theories to the dynamic modern shopping street, into a truly twentieth-century architecture.

must know
Expressionism
After the First World War many architects felt that Europe had changed irrevocably, and many, particularly in Germany, began to experiment with designs for buildings that had unusual and unhistorical forms. These projects were largely unbuilt, but include Mendelsohn's Einstein Tower. They are sometimes described as 'expressionist' architecture.

Mendelsohn's architecture

Mendelsohn was born in East Prussia, now part of Russia, in 1887. At the end of the First World War he returned to architectural practice, establishing an office which in time became the largest in Germany. In 1920 he designed an astrophysical laboratory and observatory in Potsdam outside Berlin for the Einstein Institute. With its curvaceous forms, the building appears almost to be moving: the idea was that just as Einstein's universe broke away from the stable mathematical form of Newton's, so the Einstein Tower would create a sense of restless energy and mystery.

Some of the large shops designed by Mendelsohn in the 1920s used electric light, streamlined walls, curved glass and dynamic forms to create a totally new city experience, rejecting any known historical style. His inspiration was drawn from the streets outside – full of motorized traffic and all the noisy activities of a bustling, modern European city. His buildings also incorporated the latest technology: his own house had large French windows that could be electrically lowered into the basement. Appropriately, he designed a major cinema in Berlin which became the model for others all over the world.

Tragically, the rise of the Nazis endangered his life and limited his career. He had to leave Germany, and many of his buildings (especially those for Jewish communities) were destroyed either by the new regime or by wartime bombing. Some of his buildings survive, however, and have lost nothing of their power.

Erich Mendelsohn established his reputation with the design of this observatory tower for the Einstein Institute in Potsdam.

Einstein Tower, Potsdam, Germany, 1919-21

The tower was in fact built of brick covered with plaster, but Mendelsohn had originally envisaged it as a concrete building. It has recently been restored.

Mosse House, Berlin, Germany, 1922-3

This was a huge corner and superstructure added to the existing offices of a major newspaper publisher. It is one of the few remaining examples of Mendelsohn's work that has survived in a city centre.

The newly restored pavilion at Bexhill-on-Sea in the south of England is one of Mendelsohn's greatest surviving works.

Weizmann House, Rehovot, Israel, 1934-6

This unusual house was designed for Chaim Weizmann, a scientist who became the first president of Israel.

De la Warr Pavilion, Bexhill-on-Sea, England, 1933-5

This commission resulted from a competition for a seaside pavilion on the south coast of England. The scheme was designed in partnership with Russian-born British architect Serge Chermayeff soon after Mendelsohn was forced to leave Germany.

What happened to Mendelsohn?

After leaving Germany, Mendelsohn travelled between England and Jerusalem, and finally settled in the United States. Although he did design a small number of buildings there and also taught at the University of California, he lived only for a few years more before dying in 1953.

His ideas, however, have lived on. Many architects from the mid-twentieth century have tried to turn their buildings into evocations of the excitements and conflicts of modern city life without copying the appearance of Mendelsohn's buildings. The British group of architects called Archigram (1960-75), which is sometimes associated with the Pop Art movement of the 1960s, designed a futuristic, mechanized project of this kind called 'Plug-in City'. In recent years the Dutch architect Rem Koolhaas, of the Office for Metropolitan Architecture, has also incorporated this approach into his work.

Modernism

While Mendelsohn was working in Berlin, several groups of architects across Europe were experimenting with new ideas about the aesthetics of buildings. They rejected all historical precedent and claimed to be creating a new architecture suited to the industrial age.

must know
Eileen Gray
The Irish designer Eileen Gray (1879-1976) was one of the leading proponents of the modernist style. Her best known house was a holiday villa called E-1027 she designed for herself at Roquebrune in the south of France. Her furniture designs are still popular today.

The Bauhaus

The Bauhaus is probably the best known design school in history, although it lasted for less than 15 years between the end of the First World War and its closure by the Nazis in 1933, and its architecture department operated for less than half of that time. Its best known director, Walter Gropius, turned it from a craft school with somewhat mystical ideas into a kind of research establishment, whose purpose was to calculate and define the buildings of the future in a rational way. Much Bauhaus-designed furniture such as chairs with metal frames continues to be popular to this day.

The buildings of the Bauhaus itself were designed by Gropius, and in many ways they are representative of the style associated with the school: straight lines, white walls and large windows of industrialized appearance. It seems likely that for many of the Bauhaus designers the appearance of industrialization was more important than the real thing. The reason for this was that architects wanted to express their desire to break away from the types of historical style associated with the old imperial regimes that had collapsed with the end of the War.

The Bauhaus established Gropius and Mies van der Rohe as influential teachers. In the 1930s they moved to America.

Many architects across Europe were intrigued by the work of Gropius and his circle and by the end of the 1920s there were several different places where similar ideas were being tried. Some of these designers came together to design houses for an exhibition of architecture called the Weissenhof, at Stuttgart in 1927 – an event which established the influence of the new style worldwide.

Identifying modernist architecture

The effect of the Bauhaus and its supporters was to create a new set of design elements. These features can be found in buildings everywhere from the 1920s onwards, and the resulting style is generally labelled

must know

Bauhaus survival
The Bauhaus was closed by the Nazis in 1933 but its ideas lived on. A talented group of architects in Tel Aviv, some of whom had actually studied at the school, continued to build in the same style for many more years. The city, largely planned by Scotsman Patrick Geddes, is home to more Bauhaus-style buildings than any other.

modernist, modern movement – or international modernism, because it was intended to look much the same wherever it was located. Its features can be identified easily by the following:

- flat roofs
- white plastered walls
- efficient rooms carefully designed around built-in furniture
- metal windows, often arranged in long horizontal strips
- plenty of roof terraces and balconies
- the tendency of a building to be designed as a free standing object rather than as part of a continuous urban landscape

In spite of these distinct features, the modern movement actually owed a considerable debt to historical styles. The family resemblance to the classical tradition is clear from the importance that architects gave to the overall proportions of a building

Le Corbusier's Villa Savoye, outside Paris, is one of the most influential buildings of the twentieth century.

and to the purity of its details – sometimes at considerable cost to the practicality of the resulting structure. And conversely the gothic tradition is recalled in the attempts by some other architects to emphasize the distinct uses and materials of the buildings, creating an organic effect by other means. Russian 'constructivist' architects, for example, in the exciting atmosphere after the Russian revolution, designed structures composed from differently shaped rooms assembled separately on platforms, hung with instructive banners and slogans.

Le Corbusier

Le Corbusier, the Swiss-born architect who lived from 1887–1965, was probably the twentieth-century personality who captured the imagination of designers more than any other individual. Like Frank Lloyd Wright, he was an inspired writer and self-promoter with a well developed sense of his own image; and, also like Wright, his personal architectural style changed dramatically several times without becoming inconsistent with his declared approach.

Le Corbusier, who changed his name in 1920 from Charles-Édouard Jeanneret-Gris, was a painter as much as an architect, and his buildings were primarily designed for visual effect. That is probably the secret of their worldwide success. Although he wrote enthusiastically about modern machinery and (again like Wright) designed visionary schemes for whole cities, his success lay in promoting a series of distinct aesthetic three-dimensional experiences. One of his most appealing ideas, for example, was to design buildings around changing interior vistas.

must know
Machines for living in
It was Le Corbusier who first described the modern house as 'a machine for living in'. The phrase appears in his best known book, *Towards a New Architecture*, which was published in French in 1923 and in English in 1927.

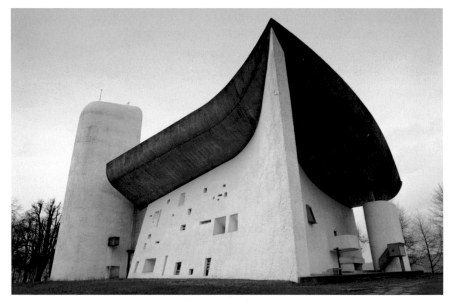

The pilgrimage chapel at Ronchamp in eastern France illustrates how Le Corbusier's later work became as much sculpture as building.

He particularly liked to use reinforced concrete because of the way it could be moulded into any shape he wanted, and then appreciated by a building's users when seen from different angles as they walked about.

Most of Le Corbusier's buildings from all periods have a number of distinct characteristics:
• a ground floor raised on concrete columns which he called *pilotis*
• a roof terrace with ornamental sculptural elements
• curved and irregularly shaped walls resting on concrete floors
• bold colour schemes using primary colours, and sometimes murals
• complicated routes through buildings using ramps and stairs: this is called 'promenade architecture'.

Le Corbusier was greatly interested in the proportions of buildings – he even invented his own proportional system – and consequently some see him as a twentieth-century classical architect. And yet on the other hand, the increasingly expressive shapes that he used for different parts of buildings relate his work equally to the gothic tradition. Perhaps it was the way in which he managed to combine the two that continues to make his work so fascinating.

The three most famous Le Corbusier buildings

Villa Savoye, Poissy, near Paris, France, 1928–31
Although extremely impractical as a home and scarcely ever used as one, the Villa Savoye has come to symbolize Le Corbusier's visionary architecture and continues to inspire.

Unité d'Habitation, Marseilles, France, 1945–52
Le Corbusier's response to chronic post-war housing shortages was to design a whole neighbourhood in the form of one gigantic sculptural block. Small-scale imitations were built all over Europe.

Chapel of Nôtre Dame-du-Haut, Ronchamp, France, 1950–5
This remarkable pilgrimage chapel, with tiny windows set into massive angled walls, was quite unlike any building ever designed. Its roof may have been inspired by the shell of a crab, but its form is reminiscent for some of a nun's cowl, a ship, or an outstretched hand.

must know
Chandigarh
From 1950 Le Corbusier worked on the design of an entire new city – the regional capital of the Punjab, India, at Chandigarh. In addition to the city layout he designed a series of imposing public buildings there including the High Court, Secretariat and Assembly.

Nordic architecture

Although the impact of French and German modernism is undeniable, it was not the only major influence on western architecture. The British in particular followed very closely developments in Denmark, Sweden and Finland.

must know
Scandinavian city halls
Copenhagen and Oslo also have fine city halls. The oldest is in Copenhagen, where the building was designed by Martin Nyrup and built between 1892–1905. That at Oslo is by Arnstein Arneberg and Magnus Poulsen (begun 1916, completed 1950); like Östberg's City Hall in Stockholm, it sits dramatically at the water's edge.

Scandinavian design

In both Denmark and Sweden, successive social-democratic-led governments fostered encouragement of contemporary design over a long period of time. They believed very strongly that it was important to invest in high quality modern housing and in pleasant, friendly public institutions such as schools, town halls, swimming pools and libraries.

The two countries escaped the ravages of the Second World War: Denmark was occupied by Germany but escaped bombardment, and Sweden was neutral. Both continued to build throughout the 1940s. As a result, many architects, particularly in war-torn Britain, looked to them for inspiration when the time finally came to start reconstruction. Even well before the war, some major public buildings such as the City Hall in Stockholm (1908–23) by Ragnar Östberg had attracted worldwide admiration.

Erik Gunnar Asplund

The Swedish architect Asplund is the best known of all twentieth-century Swedish architects. He started his career by designing in an original version of the local neo-classical style, but in 1930 became a modernist. After that date however his work never lost its humane character. His many masterpieces include:

Law Courts extension, Gothenburg, 1934-7

To the surprise of many, Asplund enlarged a seventeenth-century courtroom with an addition in the form of a modernist grid. The interior is warm and welcoming, quite unlike any typically intimidating law courts building.

The city hall at Århus is a fine example of the high quality architecture of mid-twentieth century Scandinavian public buildings.

Woodside Crematorium, Stockholm, 1915-40
Asplund worked on the design of this landscaped site and its chapels for much of his short working life, following a competition win in 1915. His final building there, the main crematorium structure, is one of the triumphs of twentieth-century monumental architecture.

Stockholm Public Library, 1918-28
Asplund's remarkable design is reminiscent of the visionary architecture of Ledoux or even Boullée, and yet the results as always are fundamentally humane in scale, atmosphere and details. The cylindrical tower above the reading room proved highly influential through Europe.

Arne Jacobsen

Arne Jacobsen has left an indelible mark on modern Danish design. In addition to his buildings he designed pieces of furniture such as the 'egg', 'ant' and 'swan' chairs still fashionable today. When working on his plans for St Catherine's College in Oxford, England, he designed every last detail of the building including the cutlery. The City Hall at Århus

must know
Eero Saarinen
The Finnish-born architect Eero Saarinen emigrated to the United States as a child in 1922. Although he died young, he designed several highly influential structures, including the crab-like TWA terminal at John F. Kennedy Airport in New York, and the 192 m (630 ft)-high Gateway Arch at St Louis, Missouri.

in Jutland, designed with Erik Møller and built from
1937–42, is a fine example of the high standards set
by Scandinavian public architecture.

Alvar Aalto

The Finnish architect Alvar Aalto is sometimes
considered to have been as dominant a figure in
twentieth-century architecture as Walter Gropius
and Le Corbusier, although his approach could not
have been more different from theirs. He valued very
greatly the use of natural materials, and imitated the
forms of nature in his work.

In 1929 Aalto designed a revolutionary sanatorium
for tuberculosis sufferers at the town of Paimo. The
building was colourful and cheerful, and Aalto
designed every detail of it with the patients' welfare
in mind. One wing of the building consists only of a
tall stack of narrow balconies, for fresh air and
sunshine. At a large house called the Villa Mairea at
Noormarkku (1938–41) Aalto mixed natural materials
and forms to create a sense of living in a forest.

Aalto characteristically used brick in a sensitive,
sculptural way. The British architect Colin St John
Wilson is a great admirer of Aalto's work, and his
best-known building, the British Library in London
(1976–98), is in some ways a tribute to the Finn.

Monumental architecture

Most major buildings of the twentieth century owe a great deal to the influence of Wright, the modernists, or the Nordic designers. Architects combined this with new ideas about materials and structure.

must know
The Festival of Britain, 1951
The years following the Second World War were austere ones in Britain, and the government agreed to sponsor a major festival of architecture and design on the south bank of the Thames in London to cheer everyone up. Several young architects first made their name at the festival.

Looking at monumental buildings

At first sight, the large monumental buildings of the mid-twentieth century often appear confusing. It is not always obvious why they look the way they do, and they do not seem to relate to any of the traditional families of design. At the same time, they have often been criticized for their ugliness and repetitiveness.

By carefully reading these buildings it soon becomes possible to identify their important characteristics, and to see how they relate to historical traditions. They may not use any directly classical or gothic forms, but you can discover family likenesses between these and the work of some of the great masters of modern architecture.

Sydney Opera House, 1956–73

Jørn Utzon, a Danish architect, created one of the great icons of the modern world with this remarkable building. The references here are to the soaring vaults of the gothic cathedral, but this time they are used symbolically to inspire feelings of exaltation rather than merely to roof the structure.

National Assembly Building, Dacca, Bangladesh, 1962–83

Louis Kahn was born in Estonia in 1901 but spent most of his life as an architect and teacher in Philadelphia.

His buildings often have massive walls pierced by small geometrical windows, creating powerful effects in light and shade. This parliament building, which was inspired by the monumental architecture of pre-Greek civilizations, is perhaps the twentieth century's answer to the Palace of Westminster.

The British Library, designed by Colin St John Wilson, is a tribute to Nordic architecture and in particular to Aalto.

Yamanashi press and radio centre, Kofu, Japan, 1964-7

Japanese architecture of the 1960s was enlivened by several gigantic rough concrete buildings which towered above the cities below them. Kenzo Tange was the leading exponent. These structures combined Le Corbusier's experiments with sculptural forms with Mendelsohn's engagement with the contemporary city.

New National Gallery, Berlin, 1962-8

Former Bauhaus director Ludwig Mies van der Rohe strove to perfect a very simple and apparently industrially inspired architecture, which reached its most perfect form in this gallery.

Byker Wall, Newcastle-upon-Tyne, 1969-82

Ralph Erskine, a British-born architect who settled in Sweden, made a lasting impact on modern public housing with this large residential scheme. Drawing on Scandinavian traditions of popular democracy, local residents were encouraged to participate in the design of the estate, and familiar materials were chosen for decorative balconies and porches.

must know
Totalitarian architecture
The European dictators tended to prefer the neo-classical style, which tainted it in the eyes of many young post-war designers. Only in Mussolini's Italy was modernism encouraged. Fascist architect Luigi Moretti later designed the Watergate Complex in Washington, D.C.

National Theatre, London, 1967–76

The British architect Denys Lasdun designed the
National Theatre in his characteristic style, known as
'brutalism'. His idea was that the whole of the
building should be a kind of theatre – for the
members of the public who used its terraces and
public spaces as much as for the actors on its three
stages. Lasdun's approach was derived from the
modernist interest in bold, pure shapes and complex
three-dimensional geometries.

The 'brutalist' style of the
National Theatre in London was
fashionable in Britain from the
mid-1950s to mid-1960s.

Pompidou Centre, Paris, 1971–7

Architects Renzo Piano and Richard Rogers created
this arts centre in an historic quarter of Paris by
reinterpreting several architectural traditions and
bringing them together under one roof. In particular,

Jørn Utzon's Sydney
Opera House is an
international
landmark. Like a
mediaeval cathedral
it celebrates the
excitement of
soaring vaults.

must know

New universities

The great expansion of British universities in the 1960s
provided almost unrivalled opportunities for architects to
design on a grand scale. A notable example is the
University of East Anglia, outside Norwich, which was
designed by Denys Lasdun in the form of a series of
'brutalist' ziggurats.

the interest in carefully expressing the structure of the building and its mechanical services (such as heating ducts) is derived from an enthusiastically Victorian approach to modern technology. In a sense, the building is a younger brother of the Crystal Palace of 1851.

The Pompidou Centre in Paris by Piano and Rogers is a lively 1970s interpretation of Victorian industrial architecture.

must know

Post-war expressionism
The expressionist approach to architecture underwent something of a revival after the Second World War, particularly in the work of the German architect Hans Scharoun, who designed the concert hall for the Berlin Philharmonic orchestra in 1956. Similar ideas flourished in the anti-Establishment era of the late 1960s.

Architecture since the 1970s

Architecture has been revolutionized over the last few decades. Changing attitudes to historical building traditions, a reaction to the modernist architecture of the mid-century, and an increasingly sophisticated approach to developing technologies – including the need to design for energy efficiency – have created a new way of building expressive of today.

must know
Norman Foster
The architect Norman Foster is sometimes considered to be one of Britain's greatest 'exports', having designed all over the world. His buildings include:
• Hong Kong and Shanghai Bank, Hong Kong (1979-86)
• Stansted Airport, England (1981-91)
• Carré d'Art Gallery, Nîmes, France (1985-93)
• Torre de Collserola communications tower, Barcelona, Spain (1988-92)
• Reichstag remodelling, Berlin, Germany (1992-9)

Technological architecture

Some of the most distinctively British architecture of the last few decades has returned to the triumphs of Victorian engineering for its inspiration. In particular, Richard Rogers, Norman Foster and Nicholas Grimshaw have designed buildings in which the structure is refined and expressed rather than hidden. In the spirit of Pugin as well as of more recent architects such as Jacobsen, these architects are also responsible for the design of all the details of their buildings. The results are often highly sophisticated.

Sustainable architecture

The typical office building of the 1970s was glazed across the whole of its outside walls, and relied on large amounts of electricity for heating, cooling and ventilation (sometimes simultaneously!). Today it is clear that such wastefulness cannot continue. Architects are now required by new building regulations to maximize natural resources by designing opening windows and spacious atriums to aid lighting and ventilation, and by installing higher standards of insulation than ever before.

It is not only the design of large commercial buildings that must change. In Sutton, south of London, Bill Dunster has designed a high-density residential scheme called BedZED that has reduced energy consumption to 10 per cent of that of the average suburban home. It is very likely to set an important precedent for future development.

Norman Foster's London headquarters for insurers Swiss Re at 30, St Mary's Axe combines technological sophistication with environmental awareness.

must know
Rem Koolhaas
Architect Rem Koolhaas is perhaps as well known for his provocative books as for the buildings he designs. His published work includes *Delirious New York*, *S,M,L,XL* and *The Harvard Guide to Shopping*, all of which have a cult following among architecture students and teachers.

Architecture of the computer

In the early years of modernism architects were intrigued by the possibilities of using scientific methods to design and construct their buildings. Now that the computer has become so sophisticated a design tool, this approach has reappeared and is responsible for some of the most striking buildings of recent years.

Frank Gehry has become famous throughout the world for the design of the Guggenheim museum in Bilbao, Spain (1991–7). The curves of the building were created by adapting a computing programme, Catia, which had originally been written to facilitate the design of aircraft components.

Bill Dunster's BedZED scheme at Sutton, south of London, has set new standards for energy conscious design.

The speed with which computer programming becomes ever more sophisticated is rapidly changing the appearance of buildings today. Complex three-dimensional parts can be manufactured, as well as designed, by computer. But in addition, some designers now see the world in a different way – free of the restraints imposed upon them by traditional approaches to structures. The recent Phæno Science Centre at Wolfsburg, Germany, by Zaha Hadid, is an indication of the exciting ways in which a new type of architecture may develop.

Zaha Hadid's Phæno Science Centre at Wolfsburg is an exciting example of the way computer-aided design can create new spaces.

must know

Poundbury

Prince Charles has been an outspoken proponent of traditional architectural styles in contemporary Britain. He commissioned the Luxemburg-born architect Leon Krier to design a village, Poundbury, on his land outside Dorchester in Dorset in order to demonstrate his ideas. The scheme continues to arouse controversy among architects and critics.

Today's architecture students can be more adventurous than ever before. Simon Whittle designed and helped build this complex hybrid structure.

Historicizing architecture

While new technologies are encouraging some designers to adapt to changing circumstances, others are beginning to look back at the past without feeling, as modernist architects did, that it is wrong to copy the styles of past generations. The American architect Robert Venturi is perhaps best known for questioning the ways in which modern architecture was developing in the 1960s. The result was that by the 1980s it became fairly common for designers to incorporate direct quotations from historical buildings – usually classical ones – in their designs.

This approach was known as 'post-modernism' and did not last very long. It was soon superseded by a more ambitious approach – that of recreating (externally, at least) the appearance and constructional methods of historical styles of architecture. This way of building has so far been relatively expensive because of the large amount of skilled labour required; but there is no doubt that it answers the need many people have to be surrounded by familiar and reassuring structures, as well as providing rewarding work for craftsmen.

want to know more?

Take it to the next level...
- Walls and roofs, 10
- How architects think, 176
- Buildings and cities, 182

Other sources...
- Visit a large, twentieth-century public building in your own town, and try to see if you can work out the influences behind its design.
- Make a list of the homes you know that were built in the last century, and try to categorize them: can you see in them elements of modernist design? Do they have historical elements in them, such as imitation half-timbering? Why do you think they look the way they do?
- Compare old photographs of your town from your local history library with the appearance of the streets today. What has changed? And what do you think inspired the buildings that have appeared over the last fifty years?

Further reading
- Have a look at one of the books specializing on the period:

Benton, Charlotte and others, *Erich Mendelsohn* (IFA, 1999)

Blundell Jones, Peter, *Gunnar Asplund* (Phaidon, 2006)

Curtis, William, *Modern Architecture since 1900* (Phaidon, 1996)

Frampton, Kenneth, and Schezen, Roberto, *Le Corbusier, Architect of the Twentieth Century* (Abrams, 2002)

Pehnt, Wolfgang, *Expressionist Architecture* (Thames & Hudson, 1973)

Rykwert, Joseph and Schezen, Roberto, *Louis Kahn* (Abrams, 2001)

Storrer, William Allin, *Frank Lloyd Wright: a Complete Catalog* (University of Chicago Press, 2002)

Weston, Richard, *Alvar Aalto* (Phaidon, 1995)

6 Thinking architecturally

We have looked at most of the important historical aspects of buildings, and especially at their materials and their style. This final chapter is different: it is about getting to know the people who design them and write about them. It is also about you: how you can use your skills to read unfamiliar buildings, and to talk and write about architecture in an informed and lively way.

Architecture and personality

Different types of people prefer different styles of building. And recognizing what motivates architects and critics is important to understanding their work.

must know
Architectural
personalities
Many famous architects
have had extremely
unusual personalities,
and some, such as Le
Corbusier and Frank
Lloyd Wright,
consciously cultivated
their own public image.
In 1943 the Russian-
born American writer
Ayn Rand published a
novel that described
one such architect and
his battles with an
unsympathetic world.
Called *The
Fountainhead*, it was
later turned into a
memorable film starring
Gary Cooper as the
heroic Howard Roark.

Who talks about buildings?

You now know a great deal about historical styles and how they have played an important role in creating the world around us. But as someone who is learning to read a building, you will want to go further than simply analysing what you see: you will try to discover the motives behind a new design, and to develop a sense of all the other aspects of architectural and building practice that add up to a complete picture.

Architects themselves speak very little about the general principles of the visual aspects of their designs, preferring instead to talk about down-to-earth issues such as the building's construction, its economics and the special requirements of their clients. That is probably because architects, like many artists, are better at visualizing their designs than they are at putting them into words. Although you may not realize it at first, they are often obsessed by their work, and keen to make sure that every detail is correct. In a sense, they never truly relax, because looking at every building, whether old or new, is a kind of work to them.

So possibly architects are not always the best people to talk about some of the profounder aspects of design and style. On the other hand, many people outside the design professions, such as economists

Mies van der Rohe's architecture looks industrial, but its components were often expensively hand finished. This is his New National Gallery in Berlin.

and philosophers, often write about the design of buildings as a way of exemplifying other phenomena. That is because the design of buildings is a major aspect of our lives in general, concerning everything from human nature to politics and sociology.

Human nature and personal style

You can approach the way in which people talk about architecture by thinking about the characteristics of the historic periods we have looked at. You will have noticed for example that some people prefer classical buildings and others gothic ones. Have you ever wondered why?

It does seem to be true that the two different styles have quite different underlying characteristics. The people who prefer classical architecture, with symmetrical fronts, neat columns, carefully considered proportions, and subdued building materials may well be those who prefer a rational, ordered approach to life. Some people today want to see more new buildings that are explicitly neo-classical or eighteenth-century in character. That does not mean that they want actually to return to the lifestyle of the past. But it probably does imply

must know

Architects and architecture critics
Some architects have also been architecture critics and some architecture critics have designed buildings. It is very unusual to be equally well known for both activities. A rare example of someone who did succeed in this was Adolf Loos, who both designed and wrote in Vienna at the beginning of the twentieth century. In one famous publication, called *Ornament and Crime*, he compared architectural decoration to body tattoos.

that in today's messy, crowded streets, or in a built
world they find ugly, they want to see buildings used
as a way of introducing a sense of calm and caution,
or even simply as a reminder of the aesthetic qualities
that they have enjoyed in the buildings of the past
and believe to be timeless. On the other hand, those
who prefer mediaeval-type buildings are often those
who care a great deal about the quality and variety of
craftsmanship in building, or who feel reassured by
the way that old buildings have grown organically or
express their purpose externally. It is certainly the
case that over the centuries people have chosen to
build in one historical style or another in order to
express their political or social views. You should
always remember that it is the architect's client, not
the architect, who is paying for a new building!

Understanding architecture critics

Many people who have written about architecture in
the past have also been greatly influenced by their own
personal feelings about what buildings are for. The
names of some of these writers are important, because
they crop up again and again in books and articles.

One of the most important names from the
Victorian era, for example, is that of John Ruskin,
who wrote a great deal about architecture, starting
from a book called *The Seven Lamps of Architecture* in
1849 and continuing almost as far as his death in
1900. Ruskin wrote in a very rich literary and
sometimes contradictory style and it is not always
possible to understand what exactly he meant. On
the other hand he left his readers in no doubt that
the design of buildings was important for everybody,
especially where it encapsulated what he considered

The art critic John Ruskin was the
most influential writer about
architecture in Victorian England.

to be the most important aspects of life: strength; delicacy; indeterminacy; wild creative force; human emotion and craftsmanship. Very few writers on architecture have had the impact Ruskin did, not least because one of his central achievements was to make writing and thinking about buildings a central part of contemporary culture.

Writing about architecture is not necessarily supposed to be objective. There have been a small number of writers and critics who have influenced the way people talk and write on the subject, and some of the best known of them should be mentioned because their influence can be seen in many places.

Le Corbusier and Frank Lloyd Wright both wrote several powerful and persuasive texts on architecture and the design of cities.

Sigfried Giedion was a Swiss writer who devoted himself to promoting the work of Gropius and of other modernist architects. His book *Space, Time and Architecture* appeared in 1941, and was widely read by young designers.

Lewis Mumford, American critic and author of *The Culture of Cities*, was also a believer in a rational approach to design, and was particularly concerned with the modern appearance of cities threatened by motorways and comprehensive planning systems.

Nikolaus Pevsner, a German refugee from the Nazis, is a well known name that frequently crops up when talking about architectural history. At the

must know
Buildings and the body
One theme that has been revived in architectural criticism is the idea that the design of classical and neo-classical architecture was closely linked to the proportions of the body, and represents the character of human beings. This concept is now particularly associated with the historian Joseph Rykwert and his many former students.

German-born Nikolaus Pevsner established architectural criticism as an important academic pursuit in Britain. The Pevsner Architectural Guides are today indispensable.

time when Pevsner arrived in England in the 1930s, architectural criticism was more of a hobby than a profession, and Pevsner's aim was to introduce methodology and to some extent academic dogma into writing about buildings. He is best known for having launched the series of exhaustive guide books to English counties known today as the Pevsner Architectural Guides and which can be found in any public library. These give accurate information about all buildings of special interest throughout the British Isles, and anyone who wants to find out more about a particular structure should always start their search there.

Pevsner is also associated, however, with a distinct way of looking at and analysing buildings. When writing in the 1930s, he believed that for about the last 100 years architecture had been moving towards simplicity and scientific rationality, and therefore buildings that exhibited these tendencies were more important than ones that did not. He therefore directed attention towards the modernist architects at the cost even of those, such as Edwin Lutyens, who had in their day been among the most celebrated architects in the world.

The idea that architecture has continually been developing in a fixed direction has been a very significant one, and the writing of some critics only makes sense if you bear that in mind, for some of the most prominent critics and historians internationally from the 1950s up to the 1970s took this view:

Reyner Banham, was one of these. He was the author of *Theory and Design in the First Machine Age*, and of *The Architecture of the Well Tempered Environment*. It can be seen that this type of writing about architecture has often been associated with a particular political view – one that sees society inexorably progressing towards social equality and systematic technological development.

Bruno Zevi, an Italian critic who had been a student at Harvard University during Walter Gropius' influential early years there, shared some of Banham's views but promoted an organic approach to design.

Because the idea that architecture could be judged by whether it was progressive or politically desirable had become so widespread throughout western society by the end of the 1970s, the work of the English architectural historian **David Watkin** is particularly important. His *Morality and Architecture* of 1977 suggested that the idea of progression along political or social lines is irrelevant to the creation or appreciation of good architecture; in particular he has also promoted the idea that classical architecture is in any case derived from principles of design that can endlessly renew themselves, and so criticism of it on the basis that it does not 'progress' is necessarily flawed.

How architects think

Architects usually start designing by drawing plans, and they use words in a particular way to describe their work. It is important to be familiar with these basic terms and to recognize their historical implications.

Why is a plan so important to architects?

Given that it is the impact of a building from the outside that seems so important, you might well wonder why architects give so much attention to its internal arrangement. The answer is that designers have always tried to get the plan of a building right before they attempt the design of its external walls.

Some reasons for this are obvious; others less so. First of all, a client will tell their architect how much money is available for the building, and the architect will be able to work out from this what the final built area that the client can afford will be. So usually the first stage in any design process is for the architect to take out squared paper and sketch the proposed rooms as rectangles of the right sizes. It is still easier to do this in the old-fashioned way with a pencil, but no doubt increased familiarity with digital technology will change this in time. Secondly, some overall building shapes are distinctly cheaper than others: by designing simple roofs that cover as much of the building as possible, by minimizing external walls, and by grouping the plumbing together in one general zone, the architect may be able to save money that can be spent on better quality materials or eye-catching features. Thirdly, the view or the

carving structural timberwork in a decorative way, and simply attaching ornaments to a building.

Interestingly, you will discover that today's architectural magazines make great use of terms and concepts that were devised in the nineteenth century, and often choose to 'take sides' when discussing buildings.

Architects have traditionally distinguished between decoration that is applied to a building, and ornament that results from cutting into or moulding its essential structure.

must know

Architectural journals
The leading international architectural journals have different points of view when choosing which buildings to promote. Some, such as Britain's *Architectural Review*, have a long tradition of supporting quality craftsmanship as well as the ideals of modernism. The American *Architectural Record* was, on the other hand, a strong supporter of post-modernism.

Buildings and cities

We have seen why buildings look the way they do. What happens when a new building is proposed for an existing street? How is its appearance judged – and does architectural design affect town planning?

What town planning is about

In Britain and those countries which have been influenced by British politics, town planning is in fact very little related to the design of buildings and it is unusual for town planners in public authorities to have qualified as architects. But wherever you are, town planning is principally to do with debating and resolving conflicts between different interest groups: those who own land, and those who use it, for example; or those who have cars as against those who do not. That is why the design of buildings plays so little a part in town planning in general.

One exception is the design of private houses: in general, it is the duty of the planning authority to protect the general residential quality – the 'amenity', as it is usually called – of a certain area. The result is that it can be very difficult to gain

Opinions change over time about the appeal of traditional housing, and yesterday's slums can become tomorrow's desirable residences.

permission to build a house which looks quite
different from its neighbours. The planners are
unlikely to be making an aesthetic decision: they are
much more likely to be trying to maintain the current
'amenity' and thus reduce potential conflict with
other residents. By contrast there has sometimes
been surprisingly little comment by planning
departments about the design of office or retail
buildings in crowded town centres.

Planning and conservation

There is very often a degree of conflict where the
protection of an old building is concerned in any
location. Some will try to keep an old building
because of its inherently attractive visual qualities;
others value it because of its use or its historical
connotations. On the other hand, the owner of the
building will feel deprived of their investment if they
cannot rebuild it as they please.

It is interesting that, like architectural criticism in
general, attitudes to the preservation of historic
buildings are as often as much to do with emotional
attitudes to the style of a building as they are to do
with practical or economic questions. People will

Plans for the London 2012 Olympics reflect the work of the most adventurous of today's architects.

The demolition of the historic propylaeum or 'arch' at Euston Station in London caused an outcry that transformed attitudes to building conservation.

sometimes support the retention of a building or of an entire area because of the associations that place has for them. It is also true that the arguments for preserving nineteenth-century buildings are often couched in different terms from those which defend eighteenth-century ones. The supporters of nineteenth-century buildings tend to emphasize their historical importance, whereas the supporters of Georgian ones prefer to concentrate on their aesthetic qualities.

These are attitudes which change from time to time. Many people appreciate the neat unbroken street fronts of Georgian cities today, but at certain times in the past they have been considered extremely ugly. There is a debate among politicians today about whether traditional nineteenth-century

must know

The Society for the Protection of Ancient Buildings (SPAB)

SPAB was founded in 1877 by the English designer William Morris in order to protect historic buildings from enthusiastic over-restoration by Victorian architects. It still exists as an amenity society and should be consulted when works are planned to a pre-eighteenth-century building.

must know

Architectural education

To become an architect requires longer than average training for a professional. In Britain and the US, a student must study full time for five years and must train with an architectural practice for at least a further two. In some countries, such as Spain, the process is even longer.

streets of terraced houses should be demolished because of the low standards of construction they were built with in the first place, or whether they should be retained and restored because of the fact that for many people they represent a secure and welcoming type of home.

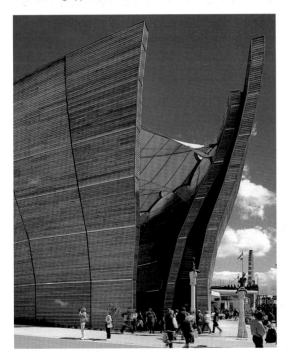

International exhibitions allow architects to demonstrate new ideas. This Hungarian Pavilion at the 2000 Expo was designed by György Vadász.

must know

The conservation movement

The growth of bodies that campaign against the demolition of historic buildings has been one of the major changes in planning history in western countries over the last forty years.

Buildings and cities | 185

Using your knowledge

Reading a building is rewarding and enjoyable. Knowing what to look for, and learning how to talk about and compare buildings, are useful keys to modern life. Now is the time to put your skills to a practical test.

must know
Architecture
Schools
Students at architecture schools spend most of their time working in teams on design projects. The emphasis is as much on creativity as on practicality. They must also learn about architectural history and building technology.

What you can do now you can read a building

When you see an interesting building for the first time and you want to describe it, there are five basic questions that you should always try to answer:

- What *exactly* does it look like?
- What was the building intended for?
- How are the materials used?
- How do I walk through the building?
- How does the building relate to its immediate context?

But as you know by now, these questions are only the beginning. From here onwards, analysing architecture becomes more of a personal matter. You will need to think about what types of style or form attract you personally – and why. Is it because some features of buildings remind you of your childhood, or a holiday abroad? Do buildings that appear historical attract you, or do you prefer more indefinable ones? Should an addition to an old building copy the style of the old one, or not? Should the interior of a building reflect the design of the exterior? What do you think about the use made of architecture in films? What do you think about the designs for large public projects, such as the buildings for the next London Olympics, and why do you think they look as they do? What connections can you make between the building you are looking at and stories you have read, or historical episodes you have known about? What kind of decoration is worth paying for, and what is not?

It is clear that questions like these do not necessarily have clear answers. That is why modern design is often described as being full of conflicts. The answers you give will say as much about you as about the buildings themselves. That is what makes architectural criticism so varied. But the one thing that is certain is that now you have learned to read a building, you will find that you know so much more not only about the buildings themselves, but about the whole of life and society around you.

want to know more?
- **Familes of design, 42**
- **Augustus Pugin, 126**
- **Le Corbusier, 149**

Other sources...
- To find out the date and the architect of a historic building that interests you, look for the Pevsner Architectural Guides in your local library.
- Find out about the national amenity societies that champion the conservation of historic buildings: the Society for the Protection of Ancient Buildings (SPAB); the Georgian Group; the Victorian Society; and the Twentieth Century Society.
- Compare the style and policies of different architectural magazines: in Britain, try the *Architectural Review*, *Architecture Today*, or *Building Design*.

Further reading

Jencks, Charles, *Modern Movements in Architecture* (Penguin, 1973)
Pevsner, Nikolaus, *Pioneers of Modern Design: from William Morris to Walter Gropius* (Yale University Press, 2005)
Stevens Curl, James, *A Dictionary of Architecture and Landscape Architecture* (Oxford University Press, 2006)
Watkin, David, *A History of Western Architecture* (Laurence King, 2005)
Watkin, David, *Morality and Architecture* (Oxford University Press, 1977)

Want to know more?

Picture credits 8 Nick Woodford/ Alamy, 11 Herbie Springer/ Alamy, 12 Steve Hamblin/ Alamy, 14 Edifice/ Philippa Lewis, 17 Neil McAllister/ Alamy, 18 David Lawrence/ Alamy, 19 Nigel Reed/ Alamy, 20 Neil McAllistair/ Alamy, 21 Edifice/ Philippa Lewis, 23 Andy Marshall/ Alamy, 24 Geoff de Feu/ Alamy, 25 Jupiterimages, 26 Chris Hammond/ Alamy, 28 NTPL/ Bill Batten, 31 Image Source/ Alamy, 38 Edifice/ Caroline Knight, 40 Thinkstock/ Alamy, 45 Kristi J. Black/ Corbis, 46 Top right: David Newham/ Alamy, Bottom left: Comstock/ Corbis, 47 Jupiterimages, 48 TongRo Image Stock/ Brand X/ Corbis, 49 Wend Images/ Alamy, 50 Jupiterimages, 53 Diomedia/ Alamy, 54 Jupiterimages, 55 Bill Brooks/ Alamy, 57 Edifice/ Philippa Lewis, 59 Edifice/ Gillian Darley, 61 Globe Exposure/ Alamy, 64 Donald Corner & Jenny Young / GreatBuildings.com, 65 Ben Ramos/ Alamy, 67 Hulton Archive/ Hulton Archive/ Getty Images, 68 Author's Image/ Alamy, 69 Peter Blundell Jones, 72 Tom Grill/ Corbis, 77 Corbis, 79 Douglas Schwartz/ Corbis, 81 Fotosonline/ Alamy, 83 David Martyn Hughes/ Alamy, 85 Glyn Thomas/ Alamy, 86 Adrian Sherratt/ Alamy, 87 Werner Otto/ Alamy, 88 James Kerr/ Alamy, 89 David Gowans/ Alamy, 91 Nigel Reed/ Alamy, 92 Nigel Hicks/ Alamy, 93 Conway Library, Courtauld Institute of Art Gallery, London, 95 Martin Bond/ Alamy, 97 Glenn Harper/ Alamy, 98 Rob Rayworth/ Alamy, 100 Pats Vigors, 101 Image Source/ Corbis, 104 James Kerr/ Alamy, 107 PictureNet Corporation/ Corbis, 108 image100/ Corbis, 111 Robert Harding Picture Library Ltd/ Alamy, 113 Jupiterimages, 116 NTPL/ Andreas von Einsiedel, 119 Peter Titmuss/ Alamy, 121 Hulton Archive/ Hulton Archive/ Getty Images, 122 Mark Karrass/ Corbis, 123 Conway Library, Courtauld Institute of Art Gallery, London, photograph by James Austin, 125 Jupiterimages, 126 Tiles & Architectural Ceramics Society, 127 The Landmark Trust, 128 britainonview/Ingrid Rasmussen, 129 Steve Hamblin/ Alamy, 130 Edifice/ Philippa Lewis, 132 NTPL/ Andrew Butler, 133 Martin Charles, 134 Urbanmyth/ Alamy, 136 Directphoto.org/ Alamy, 139 Conway Library, Courtauld Institute of Art Gallery, London, 140 Jon Arnold Images/ Alamy, 141 Top left: Courtesy of Western Pennsylvania Conservancy, Bottom right: Jupiterimages, 143 Harald Woeste/ Alamy, 144 Duncan McNeill/ Alamy, 147 Bildarchiv Monheim GmbH/ Alamy, 148 Edifice/ Adrian Forty, 150 Jon Arnold Images/ Alamy, 153 Conway Library, Courtauld Institute of Art Gallery, London, 157 Roy Lawe/ Alamy, 159 Adams Picture Library t/a apl / Alamy, 160 Jupiterimages, 161 ImageShop/ Corbis, 163 Adams Picture Library t/a apl / Alamy, 164 Zedfactory, 165 Werner Huthmacher, Berlin, 166 Simon Whittle, 168 Imageshop/ Alamy, 171 Urbanmyth/ Alamy, 172 Lebrecht Music and Arts Photo Library/ Alamy, 174 Evening Standard/ Hulton Archive/ Getty Images, 177 Quinlan & Francis Terry Architects, 178 Top left: Edmund Sumner, Bottom: Edward Cullinan Architects, 179 Comstock Select/ Corbis, 180 Hulton Archive/ Hulton Archive/ Getty Images, 181 Carl & Ann Purcell/ Corbis, 182 Mick Broughton/ Alamy, 184 Top right: www.london2012.org, Middle left: Central Press/ Hulton Archive/ Getty Images, 185 György Vadász/ Hungarian Embassy

Glossary

Aisle A continuous space through a building, usually referring to the areas either side of a church nave.
Architrave The term normally used in classical and neo-classical architecture for a beam or lintel. It also refers to ornamental mouldings which mask the junction between a door or window frame and the wall.
Arts and crafts A British movement with roots in the 1860s and which by the 1880s had become a major direction in architectural design. Arts and crafts designers insisted on high-quality workmanship and combined different elements of historical design.
Ashlar Masonry cut neatly into rectangular blocks.

Baroque A neo-classical style characterized by illusionistic decoration and complex internal geometries.
Bay A vertical division of a building.
Bay window A projecting window.
Bow window A projecting window that is rounded in plan.
Box frame A type of construction in which the whole of the frame forms a continuous part of the structure.
Brutalism A style fashionable in Britain in the 1950s and 1960s that used large masses of rough concrete to create sculptural buildings.
Buttress A masonry projection added to a wall to stiffen it.

Capital The decorative head of a column.
Cast iron Iron cast from moulds, usually industrially after the Industrial Revolution. It is strong in compression and weak in tension.
Chancel The eastern part of a church, immediately around the altar or high altar.
Clerestorey The upper part of a wall, usually of a church nave, with windows allowing light in from outside.
Colonnade A row of columns.
Composite A Roman order with capitals that combined the Corinthian leaves with Ionic volutes.
Corinthian The most ornamental of the Greek orders, characterized by capitals carved with acanthus leaves.
Cornice Any topmost decorative moulding in any material.
Course A horizontal layer of masonry in a building.
Crocket A carved ornament, usually imitating foliage, on a gothic structure.
Cruck houses Houses built from pairs of large timbers tied together to form simple trusses.

Dentils Tooth-like projections, usually forming a row in an entablature.

Doric The most plain of the Greek orders, characterized by a sturdy fluted column and a simple cushion-like capital.
Elevation An accurate two-dimensional view of a wall of a building.
English bond Brickwork in which there are separate courses for headers and stretchers.
Entablature The whole of a decorative band around the top of a classical building or of one of its major parts.
Entasis The swelling around the centre of a column to make it appear robust.
Expressionism A style of European design mainly associated with the period after the First World War. It abandoned straight lines and conventional shapes for dream-like structures of which a few were built.

Facade A special elevation.
Fan vault A highly decorative vault apparently made up of masonry carved in the form of cones and half cones with convex sides.
Flemish bond Brickwork in which the headers and stretchers are laid alternately in each course.
Flute A vertical channel carved onto a column, usually elliptical in section.
Flying buttress A masonry column placed away from a wall but part of a structural system intended to stiffen it.
Frieze A decorated horizontal band around a building.
Functionalism Architectural design which gives the impression that a building was designed strictly in accordance with its functional requirements.

Gable A raised part of a wall, usually triangular, under the roof.
Gothic revival The renewed interest in mediaeval design that characterizes Britain, and to some extent other countries, in the mid-nineteenth century.
Granite A dense igneous stone formed from cooled molten lava.
Groin vault A vault that has unembellished junctions with cross vaults.

Header The short side of a brick.

Ionic The Greek order best characterized by capitals ornamented with volutes.

Jettying A projection on an upper floor of a timber-framed house.

Lierne vault A rib vault with additional stone ribs that run between the main ones.

Glossary

Limestone A common building material consisting mainly of calcium carbonate and usually with a rich fossil content.

Metope A plain or sculptural panel in a frieze.
Modernism A style originating in central Europe in the 1920s which insisted on unrelieved white walls, industrialized units, no decoration, and a scientific or logical approach to design. The definition of the style broadens somewhat over subsequent decades.

Nave The main area of a church designated for worshippers, to the west of the chancel.

Ogee An S-shaped moulding in any material.
Open plan A layout with few permanent dividing walls.
Order One of a family of building styles in classical architecture. The three Greek orders were the Doric, the Ionic and the Corinthian, and the two major Roman ones were the Tuscan and the Composite.
Organic architecture A way of designing that respects landscape, uses natural materials, imitates natural patterns of growth and can express the functions of a building in a distinct way.
Oriel window A window that projects from an upper storey.
Ornament Decoration applied to a structure.

Palladian A building or ornament in the style of the Italian architect Andrea Palladio (1508–80).
Pediment The triangular area of masonry below the roof at the end of a Greek temple, often imitated or miniaturized in classical and neo-classical buildings.
Plan The layout of a building – actually a view of a horizontal slice through it.
Post-modernism A way of designing which rejects the dogmatic approach to style associated with any kind of modernism.
Purlin A structural element that runs horizontally across the rafters.

Rafter A structural element that connects the ridge with the wallplate.
Renaissance The revival of classical learning and architecture that began in fifteenth-century Florence.
Render A plaster-based or plaster-like wall covering, usually dense and hard.
Rib vault A vault that has masonry ribs along its junctions with adjoining vaults.
Ridge The topmost horizontal structural element of a pitched roof.

Rubble Irregular pieces of masonry built into a wall.

Section A view of a vertical slice through a building or an object.
Storey The horizontal division of a building between floors.
Stretcher The long side of a brick.
Sustainable design Architectural design that minimizes the destructive impact on the environment of the construction and maintenance of a building.

Tracery Stone cut into ornamental panels, usually for glazing in church windows.
Triforium An aisle at a high level in a large church.
Triglyphs Ornamental panels cut into the form of three upright bars, associated with the Doric order.
Truss A combination of pieces of timber or metalwork to form a vertical element in a rigid structural frame.
Tuscan The most plain of the two major Roman orders.

Vault A length of an arched masonry ceiling.
Volutes The ornamental head of an Ionic column that resembles the handset of an old-fashioned telephone.

Wallplate The horizontal structural element of a roof running along the top of a wall.
Wattle and daub A method of infilling panels in a framed structure using woven twigs and rods smeared with a thick coating of clay or similar materials.
Workhouse Before 1834, a place that dispensed local assistance to the poor and unemployed; after 1834, a kind of prison for the same people.
Wrought iron Iron shaped when hot by hand-held tools.

A comprehensive list of architectural terms can be found in James Stevens Curl, *A Dictionary of Architecture and Landscape Architecture* (Oxford University Press, 2006)

Index

◌ **Collins** need to know?

Look out for these recent titles in Collins' practical and accessible need to know? series.

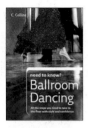    

 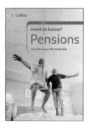   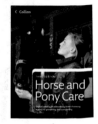

Other titles in the series:

To order any of these titles, please telephone 0870 787 1732 quoting reference 263H. For further information about all Collins books, visit our website: www.collins.co.uk